# Politics in America

## .....and how to fix it.

## Chris Rice

These are the thoughts and views from an American taxpayer. I am also a person who has grown increasingly disenchanted with the current state of affairs in Washington D.C. I still care about this country. I have decided to write this book to try and change the politics and the politicians in this country.

authorHOUSE®

*AuthorHouse*™
*1663 Liberty Drive*
*Bloomington, IN 47403*
*www.authorhouse.com*
*Phone: 1-800-839-8640*

*First published by AuthorHouse 3/25/2010*

*ISBN: 978-1-4490-9937-4 (e)*
*ISBN: 978-1-4490-9936-7 (sc)*
*ISBN: 978-1-4490-9935-0 (hc)*

*Library of Congress Control Number: 2010903482*

*Printed in the United States of America*
*Bloomington, Indiana*

*This book is printed on acid-free paper.*

# Prologue

The thoughts, ramblings, and rants from all 3 sides, the left, the right, and poor ol' me in the middle.

I know that I tend to jump from one subject matter to the next sometimes in this book more than I should, and sometimes back to the previous one. But as I have stated before, these are my thoughts and ramblings and rants. This book is not meant to offend any particular person or groups of people. But I also know that it will offend people and certain groups of people. Politicians in Washington D.C. tend to offend many people in this country on a regular basis. So with that in mind, I really don't have a problem with offending the politicians and their politics in Washington D.C.

**Good deeds from a man are only trumped
by good deeds from men.**

Chris Rice, 2010

**Good Times and Rich's and Son-of-a-Bitch's,
I've Seen More Than I Can Recall.**

(Quoted from a Jimmy Buffett song)

**Do not Confront Me with My Failures,
I Have Not Forgotten Them.**

(Quoted from a Jackson Browne song)

# Contents

1.  About Me.                                          1

2.  The Democrats.                                    13

3.  The Republicans.                                  19

4.  The News Media.                                   25

5.  Illegal Immigration and Race Relations.          27

6.  States Rights.                                    33

7.  Social Security.                                  37

8.  Crime                                             41

9.  Creating Jobs.                                    47

10. If I were the President.                          53

11. Foreign Policy.                                   65

12. Ramblings and Rants.                              73

Hopefully this will turn into a real eye opening political movement book. I'm trying to decide who should play me in the movie as well.

# Chapter 1.

# About Me.

To be a true Southerner, one does not necessarily have to be born in the Deep South or even in the South at all. To be a true Southern Gentleman, a man needs to be respectful of others, especially to women, children, and their elders. Respect is never given to anyone. It has to be earned. But once earned, it takes something colossal to be taken away from someone.

There is a huge difference in being respectful to someone, and having respect for someone.

They must be courageous, proud of who they are, and very proud of their Country and their home State. You must be tolerant of others, especially those who do not agree with you.

You have to carry yourself proudly, but not be arrogant. Like I said you don't have to be born in the South to have these traits, but it seems like it sure does help. But of course, I was born in the Deep South, and

I am very proud of that fact, and even more so, by saying I was born in the Great State of Georgia, in the year of 1963.

Calling me a gentleman may be one of the biggest over statements of all time. By the way, I'm guessing you could get fairly long odds on that in Vegas.

Being a Southerner anymore is simply a state of mind, and life can be hard for us. It's inside your mind, and it's in your heart, and it's in your deepest soul. To be a Southern White Man at this time in history is even harder. We have the least amount of rights of anyone in this country. Every other person, of every other color gets preference ahead of us. I can't speak for every other white man in America, but I have never owned any slaves. But it does seem like I am the one paying for white people owning slaves 150 plus years ago. I was not even around when slavery was legal, and I'm pretty sure no one else is either.

We have been typecast as being backwards, clumsy, awkward, and very uneducated, and if you believe the media and the Democrats, very racist. At times, 1963 yes this has been the case for some, but for the most part very untrue. Another thing a lot of people seem to forget, a lot of things people call racist was legal back then. I'm not saying right or wrong, I'm saying it was not illegal for people, schools, restaurants, and a lot of other places to be segregated.

Changes like that have to come slowly for some people. If a person owned their own business and wanted to limit it to only white people or to only black people, I don't really care. People it's 2010, not 1963!

Let's take me as an example. I'm 47, White, decent house with a mortgage, truck and a car, divorced, grandfather, full head of hair, decent job. I make pretty good money, around 100k a year, and I have a little money in the bank, around 50,000 dollars. Not rich by today's standard of rich by any means, but very well off if you don't have any of the things I mentioned. There were many years I did not have them either.

People from the South seem to be very firm in their beliefs, whatever they may be. I know I am. Things such as politics, we tend to be very Republican or very Democrat. I happen to know people who I call friends of both persuasions.

I am not a smart person by anyone's standard. I did not even finish high school. I dropped out because I knew I was not a college type person, and my living arrangements were not geared for me going to college. But for the most important reason's, I was not smart enough and I did not care and or know enough to even want to go to college. A paycheck beat the hell out of a report card.

I learned very early in life that Kroger would cash a paycheck, but not a report card.

Depending on what part of my life you wanted to put under a microscope, 0-10 or 10-18 or 18-23 or 23-29- or 29-40 or 40-47 those are just kind of milestones years for me. But it would depend which set of years you look at as to what kind of person that you would think I was.

If you took 0-10 years old, you would be talking about the kid from a very disjointed family. My parents divorced when I was a little past 1 year old. My father had received custody of my brother and myself. My brother was about 3 when they divorced.

The story I have always heard was that my mother gave up custody of us for a new car.

My father worked construction for a living. That means doing a lot of traveling. Well anyway he was on a job, staying at a boardinghouse and he met the woman who was running it. She had 4 kids from 2 different men. They decide to basically become the Brady Bunch way before they ever decided to have a television show about them. So now

I am the youngest of 6 kids, I now have 2 older step-brothers and 2 older step-sisters. I caught a lot of crap from them, and I had a lot of hand-me-downs.

Of course this was not your average fairy tale, even though something I think all we could agree on was the fact that we all had, and hated the evil mother/step-mother. Even her kids didn't like her. She was mean to all of us, but I do think my brother and I took the worst of it. There's no point in getting into the many beatings we all took, many for the slightest of transgressions. How bad can a 6 year old be? I'll put it this way, I was in the first grade, and I only missed 1 day of school that year. It was because I had a cut above my eye from getting backhanded across the room for not taking the clothes out of the washing machine and putting them in the dryer fast enough. Back then kids had chores before and after school.

Then I was 10 years old and my life changed again. 2 ½ weeks before my 11th birthday my father died in a car wreck coming home from work. That's a tough one for a 10 year old boy. My dad was a pretty good guy. He did drink a lot, but he never hit or abused any of us.

Now getting older myself and working construction also, I can understand why he drank. Between construction work and the evil bitch that he married. He was even good to the step-brothers and step-sisters. We all used to go hunting and fishing and camping a lot. The oldest step-brother was 16 almost 17 when my dad died.

But when he had turned 16, my dad had gotten him a car, not new but a decent Mustang. The next oldest step-brother had gotten a small motorcycle a year or two earlier. My dad dying was hard on all of us kids.

My Grandfather who had already had 1 heart attack was threatened by my step-mother, that if he didn't turn over a life insurance policy worth 40,000 dollars to her that she was going to drop my brother and I off on their doorstep that very day. It was a policy that my dad had set aside for my brother and myself for when we turned 18 we could have a good start at life. He had purchased it way before they had even met and before they had gotten married.

This is after she had already gotten a couple of other life insurance policies from his death. One paid off the house, one was for 100,000 dollars, and at least one more for 50,000 dollars. My Grandfather once told me that he regretted ever giving in to her, and that he was sorry that he had done it. I told him that he should never be sorry for doing what he thought at the time was the right thing to do. I told him that since I never got it, it was not something I had missed. I guess I was about 17 when he told me about it, and knowing most 18 year olds I would have just blown it on a car and or girls.

Both of the step-brothers got brand new cars, as well as the step-sisters after my dad died.

When my older brother turned 16 he ran away, and after he came back, he was sent to live with my grand-parents. When I was 15 I too was sent to live with my Grand-parents also.

If you took the ages of 18-23, I would be a poster child for the Democrats. In the Army at 18, I had nothing really else to do at the time. I was discharged from the Army at 20 with nowhere to go. I looked up my mother whom I had not seen in about 10 years. She and my father had divorced when I was less than 2 years old, my father had been given custody of me. She was living in the Houston Texas area. Well let's just say that things did not work out too well after a month or 2, and I headed back to Georgia.

I had loaned her all the money I had, a little over a thousand dollars. I had just received my tax refund. She wrote me a note telling me that she didn't think it was going to work out, "me living with her". Then she bought me a bus ticket back to Georgia.

I moved in with a relative that I still knew where they lived. I then received a letter from my mother's lawyer. She had filed bankruptcy, and filed against me what she had borrowed from me.

I stayed with an Aunt and Uncle in Georgia for a couple of months, and decided that this was not going anywhere. So I took a map of Georgia, opened it up, closed my eyes, and pointed to a spot on the map and asked them if they could take me there on the upcoming weekend.

I had 78 dollars in my pocket, my army duffle bag, my army sleeping bag, a small pup-tent, about 5 old uniforms and 2 pair of jeans, a pair of sneakers and a pair of Army boots. I went to a pawn shop and pawned a couple of uniforms and a few other things, and bought a shotgun and a fishing pole. I bought them for hunting and fishing, and I was planning on living off of the land.

They took me to the town like I asked, and we had lunch, and I then had them drop me off on the side of the road, next to a river in North Georgia at a boiled-peanut stand.

I camped in the woods next to the river that first night. I had some canned goods, but it had rained and anything to make a fire with was wet. So I had a can of cold pork-n-beans that night for dinner. It got cold that night, into the lower-40's I thought I was going to freeze to death.

Anyway the next day I had just about had enough, and decided to ask the people at the peanut stand for a ride into town. I was going to call my uncle who dropped me off and ask if I could come back for awhile.

I didn't want to, but thought I had to. As I was walking along the river going to the peanut stand my life changed again. I started talking to a person, who as it turned out was living under the bridge. He asked me if I was on the road, and then one thing led to another, and he had a good size tent and a heater so I agreed and moved in under the bridge. I have never needed to make that phone call again in my life.

I lived under that bridge for almost a year. I met some of his friends who were local residents of the town, and we became good friends. The friends were 3 brothers who had grown up in the local town.

They were just 3 good ol' boys to the core, country boys, nothing fancy. We fished, hunted, drank beer, played the guitar, and I enjoyed the hell out of it.

I had no worries, life was good. I bathed in the river, washed my clothes there too. I would help campers out with stuff like setting up their tents, or helping them launch their canoes, and things like that, they would give me a few bucks now and then. I changed a few flat tires for people, sometimes they would give me 5 maybe 10 dollars. I never did ask them for money, they always offered it. I did something nice for them they did something nice for me. It was just enough for some food, and sometimes townspeople would drop off food also.

We would pan for gold in the river, and even find a little every now and then. When we needed food, or other things we would sell the little gold we had found in town or to campers. We are not talking gold bricks here either, I don't know if we ever made more than 20-25 dollars at any one time. But it was enough to sustain us in food, ammo, fuel for our camp stove and fuel for the heater when it was cold. The basic things in life for me at that time.

I did not take to stealing and robbing to survive. I had nothing to speak of, my most prized possession was a 40 dollar single shot 12 gauge shotgun.

Now you tell me, is that not the poster child for being a Democrat? A white man, homeless, a veteran, living on hand-outs, living under a bridge, no money, no job, no car, basically no family, and no prospect for any of the above. The Democrats in power today would be promising me anything for my vote. And most of the Republicans today would wonder what kind of drugs I'm hooked on and who I'm robbing or stealing from, and just hope it's not them.

But that urge to do something different was coming back to me again. I've always had that ol' traveling bone. I had saved up a few bucks by helping a friend cut some firewood and a few other odd jobs, and decided I was going to get a job and a place to stay in town.

Anyone could get hired on at one of the many chicken processing plants in the area. I was going to rent a room at a boarding house in town, but one of my friends that I had meet on the river talked me into renting a room from his sister who also worked at one of the chicken plants nearby. So I ended up renting a room in town from one of friend's family, and took a job with them at a chicken plant. Wow a few paychecks and I was rich.

I lived there a year or so, but it helped form me so much in my mind, it instilled the good ol' boy in me forever. I learned so much about myself. I learned that I could make it in this world, and I grew up. I learned that I wanted to be that friend that could bring the food and beer to my friends. But not as being better than they were, just that I could.

It is now time to jump ahead to the next age time frame. 23-29. Well after a few years back in Georgia, I thought it was time to go back and try Texas again. I called my mother, asked if I could stay with her for a couple of months, just long enough to find work and get my own place, she agreed. I guess after filing bankruptcy on your own child it's tough to say no.

A couple of nothing jobs later, and a few drinking and poker buddies, I moved from my apartment into a friend of mines apartment who had just got divorced. We figured we both could save some money. A few months later he lost his job and wanted to move back to his home town, so I said lets go. A few months later I have meet a girl, we got a kid on the way, time to get married. A few stints in jail, it's a Texas thing to get yourself a couple of felony convictions.

Now I am the perfect Democrat. I've been homeless, no money, and now a convicted felon.

There's not a lot to look forward to at this point in time. I'm sitting jail, 27 cents to my name, nobody to call for help, poor pitiful me. I get extradited back to Texas, I stand trial, and I get a 10 year sentence. I spend 18 months behind bars, before I get paroled. The wife takes me back in, mostly for the kids I think. I don't think she ever trust me again. I will say this, I did my 8 ½ years on parole without getting into anymore trouble. To me that is what parole is for, it's your 2nd chance, or in my case 3rd chance.

I now get a job in construction, starting out at the bottom, as a helper. There are not a lot of jobs out there for a convicted felon, with no high school diploma, and with no skills really.

I don't think cooking in restaurants qualifies as a special skill.

After doing this for a few years, I decide I don't really like being the low paid guy doing all of the hard work. I start paying attention to what is going on around me on the jobs. I see all of the crap from the supervisors who think they know everything. I decided I want to make more money, and I think I can do what they are doing, and most likely better than they can do it. I apply myself and finally get promoted to a foreman on a job. Yes it takes a few years, but I get my chance to either put up or shut up. This starts a 4-5 year run with many different companies, most times as a supervisor, but not always.

You take what you can get when you can get it. You try to make a name for yourself and do a good job, that's all anyone can do, or ask you to do.

By now it's 2002 and it's time to get my divorce. I take off on the road again looking for work. They call people like me in the construction business, "roadwhores". That's because we'll go anywhere and do almost anything for the job and for the money.

I have a few bucks put away by now, maybe 5,000 dollars. I have my tool box, my truck, and I've purchased a R.V. By now I'm mostly only taking supervisor jobs, but not always. Sometimes I leave out the part about being a convicted felon, but for the most part no one asks me.

It's kind of like the gay policy in the military, don't ask don't tell. Anyway I'm on another job, and I get noticed by some higher up people who work for a different company for doing a real good job. They ask me to apply to their company. I do and about 6 months later they call me for a job.

Now up until now I've been making around 20-23 dollars an hour, working as many hours as I can. This new company offers me like 46 dollars an hour. I jump all over it. I've been with them now for almost 5 years. The job I'm on right now I am making around 75 dollars an hour. The last 4 years I've made at least 105,000 a year. Last year I made around 170,000 dollars.

Now you have some of the back ground on me. I know I went through a lot of years in a quick fashion, but I wanted to get to other things. I just wanted the reader to have a basic feel for me as a person. I did not grow up with a silver spoon in my mouth. I was not even close to being a privileged child or young adult. I did hit rock bottom before I started climbing my way back up. I most likely will never be a millionaire, but I've came a long way from where I have been. If I can do it, then so can anyone else. You just have to want to better yourself, and have a better life for yourself.

As I said earlier, my parents divorced when I was less than 2 years old. My dad had custody of me and brother.

He remarried the meanest women that ever lived in the state of Georgia. I had step brothers and sisters, half brothers and sisters too, and I was the youngest. I caught a lot of crap growing up. My dad died when I was 10, and I lived the next 5 years with the wicked step-mother. She then dumped me at my Grandparent's house with a paper sack full of clothes. So I don't want to ever hear about a rough childhood. The stuff she did then, people go to jail for now-a-days.

# Chapter 2.

# The Democrats.

I'm not going to spend a lot of time or energy on either political party. Neither one of them are really worth it.

I heard or saw this quote on the internet, I do not know who said it, but to me it should be the Democrats motto, it goes something like this. "There are two ways to slice easily through life; to believe everything or to doubt everything. Both ways save us from thinking for ourselves."

I keep hearing about how the Democrats want to make everything better for everyone, "horse hockey"! They just want to be in charge. They want the poor people to stay poor so they will always have people who will want what the other person has. That is there base......Well them and people who act in movies, or try to.

This way they then can stand up and shout, see those Republicans have all this stuff and they don't care about you. See how the Republicans are always trying to keep the minorities down. The Democrats want the poor people and the minorities to then look up and say, hey maybe their right.

Guess what people, those poor people; they already knew what they didn't have. They don't need or want someone telling them what they don't have. They're just trying to let you give them a little bit more. Anyone can stand and point to someone else and say, look at all that stuff or all that money that they have. They have more than they need, they should give some of that to me. The problem with that is that the other person worked for what they have, and they want to keep it too.

I am so tired of hearing people say I can't find a job. What they need to say is this, I can't find a job that's pays me what I want to make, and will let me do whatever I want to do.

Guess what people, you don't get to start out at the top. I do not donate anything to any politician or political party ever! I think they all are crooks and liars. They are all self serving and arrogant people who only go into politics for the prestige and the money they can make….. well that and the free perks that all come at the taxpayer's expense. That is not limited to any special party, or even region of the country, and race does not even factor in it at all. One more thing everything wrong in the world is not George W. Bush's fault, so get off of it already.

The Democrats always blame the Republicans for making too much money and not sharing it with the poor people in this country. I would like to see how many millionaires that there are in each party in Congress. On this matter I side totally with the Republicans. People I've been poor, and I'm talking about really poor. The kind of poor where you don't know where you're going to sleep that night or where your next meal is coming from. If you want something more, go out and work for it. In my job, I have been able to travel, or more like, I've had to travel all over this country, and even to different countries. I've learned a few things, first nothing is free, not even freedom.

This country is the only one that I have ever seen that it does not matter to whom you were born, or in what state you were born in to, or what part of the country you were born in. On a farm, out in the sticks, inter-city, suburbs, ghetto, or even put up for adoption. This is the only country in the world, that what you become is totally 100% up to you. In most countries the status of your family will dictate what happens to you your whole life.

In my opinion that's where the United States has an advantage over all of the other countries in the world today.

There may be a couple of the European countries that it is also possible, but none I think with the opportunities of this country.

If you apply yourself in school, you can get a scholarship to a college. With a college degree of your choice you can do whatever you want to do. I don't care if you have 1 or 2 parents or even none. But the big thing here is you have to want it, and be ready to work for it. You can't sit on your ass and expect anything or everything to be given to you. You have to go out and earn it. Most people don't want a handout, but at times they sure could use a hand up.

If you keep taking handouts, you'll get accustomed to getting handouts, and then that's all you'll ever want or expect.

Republicans don't get to cocky just yet I'm not giving you a free pass either. But we will come back to you later on.

I'm writing this just after the Massachusetts Special Election where Teddies old seat just went to the Republicans. I for one never thought that would be possible. Then after the Democrats hurriedly changed their state law that they had put in place in the first place to help the

Democrats in case Kerry had beat Bush in 2004. Then they put their hand-picked Senator in there to vote the way they wanted.

No way did I think it was even a remote possibility they would lose that seat. I bet Ted Kennedy is falling off of his bar stool. I would like to quote something from the current first lady. (For the first time in my life I am proud to be an American). Pun intended.

Many people in this country were/are rightly worried about the Health Care Reform overhaul. I was/am not too concerned. I never thought they could get it past their own party. Even with all of the midnight meetings, and secret White House meetings, and voting on Christmas Eve. Jeez what a joke that was. These are the same people who have more vacation days than work days.

Yet now they stay past midnight and work weekends and on real Holidays? What's up with that? All of this with the direction and blessings from someone who can't string 2 sentences together without a teleprompter.

The Democrats were telling everyone who they could get to listen that this Health Care Reform Bill was the best thing for America since sliced bread was created. How in the hell could something that good for the whole country be so Damn important one day, then the very next day after they lose 1 Senate seat go to the back burner?

If anyone had any doubts about whether this Health Care Reform Bill was totally about partisan politics or something for the good of the country......well I hope you have your answer now.

While I'm here talking about the Democrats, I guess I need to cover the Independents in the Senate also. What a joke they are. What part of the word independent do they not understand? They're not Independents. They're not even close to being Independent. They caucus with the Democrats, and they sit on their committees. The Democrats count their vote as part of the Democratic Party. The news media even counts them as part of the super majority that the Senate had.

Hell I can't even blame the media for this, after all they always vote with/for the Democrats anyway. If either of them were from my home state, I'd try to get them arrested for impersonating a Democrat.

I would not have a problem with 100 Independent Senators. That's what they all should be. But I'll be covering more on this subject later.

I honestly do not think Congress knows how to pass any type of bill that would actually be good for the country anymore. The only items that they even debate on are things most people in this country could care less about.

Hell even the trillion dollar stimulus bill that they passed, (shoved down our throats) even by their own admission's had money for creating jobs at the end of it, if it did so at all. Almost every bill that is put forth in Congress simply has things in it that will benefit people in Congress and their buddies. Then they tried to pass a Jobs Bill, which at the last minute was tossed in the trash. It forgot only 1 thing after all of the pork projects were inserted in it......jobs for the American people.

I've been reading so many stories, blogs, and comments about the aftermath of the special election that denied the Democrats a total free pass to pass whatever legislation they want. And pass it whenever they want to pass it. They still don't get it, Obama, Nancy, Harry, and every other Democrat keep saying, we hear you... we hear you....it's all about the jobs. No it is not! It's about you idiots trying to shove things down our throat that we don't want.

The American people have had enough, we're tired of our President bowing to other people, and apologizing to other countries, we don't care who they are. Most of those other countries are someone we've bailed out big time in the past.

We're pissed off at all of Washington D.C. The American people put you there and we can take you out of there.

We're tired of politics as normal, we wanted a change, and we didn't get it. Obama has lied to America since day one. That clown Nancy and that idiot Harry don't have a clue. Nancy just wants to punish the Republicans. I guess they slighted her in a past life? Harry drew the short straw and had to be the Senate leader. I guess because no one else with the Democrats wanted to give up their seats on special committees. Pull your heads out of your ass and out of Obama's ass too.

Our Government is based on 3 separate and supposedly equal branches of Government. You're trying to make it just the Democrats house, period!

You've placed a person on the Supreme Court to try to sway things your way, which by the way, was not overly qualified to be there. That brought immense shame on your party. You've bought the Senate members, and you control the House. And one other thing, get out of bed with the unions. You people need to get back to governing for the good of the people or the good old people are going to change things for good.

Here's a question for the hardcore left-wingers, why is it alright to kill human babies before they are even born, but not alright to kill baby seals? I'm not a woman, hell I've never even dressed up like one. So I'm never going to have an abortion.

The only man, who should ever have anything to say about an abortion, would be the man who got the woman pregnant or her doctor.

# Chapter 3.

# The Republicans.

I told you guys I was coming back to you, now here it is, and you're not to going to like it either. You guys are not a lot better than the Democrats, but everyone already knows that. You've got to get off of your religious high horse. You're not doing yourselves any good by acting morally superior to everyone else. Some of you people act so self righteous it's pitiful. Then some congressman gets busted with a house page boy, or in an airport bathroom, or has an affair with a lobbyist, please give the American people a break. Try to at least keep your pants zipped up while you're in Washington D.C., or on official business, or even better, while you're an elected official.

Now for the important things in life. You have to pass laws that deal with the real problems in this country. Most of which you people in Washington D.C. have created in the first place. Problems like giving states their own rights back, bank bonuses, Wall Street corruption, insurance reform, real health care reform, illegal immigration, lobbyist, crime and crime sentencing reform, illegal drugs, campaign finance reform, creating jobs, and tax reform.

We the people...remember us? We do not want government involvement in our life!

The U.S. Government should be like a small child to us, seen but not heard. If we need you we'll call you, don't call us. We want the Government to be run like a successful business. Show us a profit. Give the states the right to make their own decisions on a lot of things.

Take abortion for example, I do not want the government paying one dollar for any women's abortion. If Alabama decides after they vote state wide to make all abortions illegal that should be up to Alabama, not Washington D.C. or some Senator from California. If Georgia decides to make abortions legal, after they vote on it state wide, then so be it.

I guess the women from Alabama would have to go to Georgia to get an abortion. That should be a decision left up to each state.

If you don't like a state law, then vote to change it, or move to another state. If the U.S. Government has to be in that picture at all, the only thing I would suggest would be this, they have to be at least 18 before they can do it, or have the parent's permission, and both parties involved, to have it done. The bottom line here is this, me being from Georgia, I do not want or need someone from California or Nevada making decisions for me. Yes there are always exceptions to everything. Those can be worked out by each state.

It does not matter what the subject is, I don't think everyone is going to be happy about anything.

Here is a real big modern day problem that has reared its ugly head lately, bank bonuses. Republicans this is so simple, you people in Washington can't see the forest because of all those damn tress. First of all about 75% of this country disagreed with all those damn bailouts.

The ones that did want it were mostly because of union related crap. They were saving their own asses. You can't bail out a company...ever! There is a thing called a monopoly, ever heard of it? Our Government used to break those up and or not allow them. Too big to fail, no such thing.

Our whole country's economy is based on if you make it better and cheaper than the other guy, you'll do well, if not, you'll fail. You simple put regulations and controls in place, say for banks. Make it like a Las Vegas casino, if they have 10 million chips in play, then need to have 10 million in cash on hand. Do the same thing to banks, if they have 10 billion in loans then they need 10 billion worth of assets at any time.

How many businesses pay out bonuses to their employees after those same employees lose 10%-50% of their net worth? None, that's how many. I'm not going to reward someone for losing my money, why are they?

I once decided to play the stock market, I invested 1000 dollars with a national firm, in about 3 months it was worth 650 dollars, I took out what was left, and never went back in. I didn't get an option of asking for a bail-out to get my money back, but I also had enough sense to not lose any more of it too. I was hoping to get one of those White Water Hillary Clinton deals. The kind of deal where you get to invest 1000 dollars and get back over 100,000 dollars, all in a couple of weeks. Jeez, those politicians sure are lucky when it comes to investing their own money. Isn't it a damn shame they can't do that when their playing monopoly with the tax-payer's money?

Government regulations and laws and controls, put them in place, and then enforce them! Then have the proper departments pay attention to them. Put laws in place to control crap like the gas price hike of 2 years ago. If the truth were to be known, the Republicans lost the election mostly because of that fact. Well that and because a black guy

ran for president, and almost 99% of the blacks voted for him. I'd also
be willing to bet around 50% of those that did vote for him do not vote
in most elections. Black voter turn-out was at a record high. It did not
matter who the Republicans ran against him they were going to lose.
Not that McCain even tried to run much of a race.

There were some Republican leaning people that I know, and we
had a few conversations about the Democrats. I asked this question to
a few of them, who would you vote for, Obama or Hillary? Almost all
got a very sick look on their faces. But overall the vote went to Hillary,
simply because Obama never said anything about anything. He simply
reads what his cronies put in front of him. He stands for nothing but
whatever he thinks the people listening to him at that time might want
to hear. With Hillary, at least people knew what kind self centered and
self serving entity they would be getting. Did anyone really listen to
Obama?

When the person running for the job of President of the United
States of America says "this is the greatest country in the world, please
join me and help me change it." What's up with that? The Democrats
haven't had their own message since JFK went in office.

Campaign finance reform, this can't be that hard people. Only an
individual should contribute to any candidate. Set a limit if you want
to, maybe then the candidates will have to campaign on the issues. Not
the person who can afford the most air time. Companies should not be
allowed, same as unions, neither should be able to donate anything.

Make lobbyist a thing of the past. If people in Congress listened
to the people they are suppose to represent, no lobby would be needed.
The only thing they do is say it louder than an individual can say it, that
and bribe and give special little perks so they get what they want. Free
plane rides, nice little vacations, "working vacations of course", hiring
the wife or kids or son-in-law to write a memo once a year for 300,000

a year. Or get someone hired on at a big time law firm. Washington, we're tired of it. Clean it up or we will clean you out.

Rewrite the tax code, make it fool proof, take out all of the damn hidden tricks that only the rich lawyers know about. Or make it a flat tax.

The way it is now, you tax us when we work for it, you tax us when we spend it, you tax us if we save it, you tax us if we invest it, you tax us if we die and still have any left over.

Start creating some jobs that stay in this country. Do away with Nafta and all that crap. Get our trade imbalance back in line, I don't think we really need all that crap from China. We make almost nothing in this country anymore. We import almost everything. There is no way you can convince me that we cannot make a pair of blue-jeans or a light bulb cheaper than what it takes to get them made in China and then shipped over here.

# Chapter 4.

# The News Media.

This will not be a very long chapter. The News Media as it is today is just not worth it.

The press needs to do their damn jobs! Quit catering to those who you're not mad at. You could be so important if you would just state the facts and leave your opinions in the trash where they belong. When I bother to watch any news, I watch Fox, at least they try to give me another point of view other than what the Democrats have told them to say, and in turn want us to hear.

There are a lot of people out there who think Fox News is a very Republican based station. I do not think so. I think that the others are just so far to the left of center that anything Fox News does say just seems so far to the right. Why don't you try being real investigative journalist for a change? Look for the facts, the real facts, not just what the Democrats think.

The way the press fell all over itself during the presidential election was pitiful. I don't care who is running, but if they run they are open to everything. I also don't care if they are black, white, yellow, or green.

I want someone who knows what the hell is going on in this country, and in the world. A half completed first term Senator is not what I'm looking for. Especially from a corrupt state like Illinois. Their politics are famous for being corrupt and underhanded. I think the only qualification needed from there to be a politician is that you're off of parole.

Also, once they get there don't coddle them. It's a hard job yes, but they wanted it. We did not go out and just pick them, they wanted it, now they got it. To keep it they need to earn it.

All of the news media shows, NBC, CBS, ABC, MSNBC, and all of the other ones out there, lost any credibility with me and a lot of other people in this country forever. They will never be able to recoup it either.

The press should be here to help keep the politicians honest. They should also be some of the first to call them out when they've done something wrong, or lied to the American people. If I were an elected official serving in Washington, I would rotate reporters from my home state to my office to help keep me in line, and to sometimes remind me what I promised the people in my state that I would or would not do.

People in Washington D.C. that are in the U.S. Government, you work for me, and every other legal citizen of this country. You do not work for unions, businesses, the NAACP, law firms, banks, Wall Street, or even the damn press. You do not work for black people, white people, or any other color person, you work for every legal citizen of this country.

# Chapter 5

# Illegal Immigration and Race Relations.

I said earlier that I would come back to Illegal immigration, well here we are. First thing, if someone wanted to migrate to this great country and after they passed all background checks and paid their fees. They would have to be able to speak English, and be encouraged to do so at all time's in Public.

Illegal immigration, please stop calling them undocumented people. They are illegal immigrates. If someone wants to come to this country, do it the right way. If they don't, they need to be arrested and shipped back to their country, along with a bill for sending them back.

First of all, after people read this I hope they are going realize that I am 100% correct. First and foremost, enforce and obey the laws that we have already written, before trying to write new ones. Why in the hell is Washington D.C. going to rewrite immigration laws, when they won't let anyone enforce the laws that we already have now?

My first appointment would be an immigration person that (I'm sorry I just cannot say czar) would follow the laws as they were intended. I would appoint Sherriff Joe from Arizona. My instructions would be clear and simple. If they are here illegally get them out and or lock them up. Once you get a full bus send them to their home country.

My definition of an illegal alien would be simple also. If you were not born here legally, or you do not have a green card, or if you were born here to illegal aliens in this country, then you are an illegal alien. Basically what I'm saying is this. If either of your parents were here illegally and you were born here, you are therefore an illegal alien.

I would put an end to the anchor baby status. Also if you commit a felony crime and certain misdemeanors, you would be deported as soon as your sentence was up, which means no early release and no parole.

If you decide to come to back to the U.S.A. after being deported for any reason, you would receive an automatic 5 year prison sentence. Second offence would double that time. All sentences for illegal aliens would be at hard labor. There would no free prison rides for them at all. Their home country would then receive a bill for services rendered, including any medical cost.

I think that might help persuade them to also help control illegal border crossings.

Now I have used some states as an example which this might hit a little close to home to. But let's face facts people. There are not a lot illegal aliens in this country from England, or Germany, or Russia, or even Canada. Most of the illegal aliens in this country are from Mexico and South America countries.

We need to stop worrying about being so damn politically correct in this country. Let's face facts, so many people, and movies, and even television can't say what they want to say for fear of offending somebody or group or cause.

And I'm not talking about the bullshit things in life either. No, it's not OK to walk down the street with a big sign that says I hate niggers, or wetbacks, or even honkies.

I also don't think its right to have only black collages or black only broadcasting stations, or black only magazines. Unless it is black owned and they receive no assistance from any state or federal government agency. I don't even care who owns it. If Bill Gates wants to open a collage for blacks only, that fine by me. If he wants to open one for whites only in another part of the same city, that too is fine by me. I don't think anyone would care.

If you want to have those things, then you have to allow white only for the same things. Neither should ever receive any kind of financial help from either state governments or from the federal government. Does it benefit black people to go to an all black collage? Do black people learn better or faster when they are only around other black people? Then perhaps white people would learn faster or better if they could go to a collage that had only white people there?

I do not care if there is an all black collage anywhere, I have absolutely no problem with that at all, or even how many there are. My problem is this, if you had an all white collage it would be the most racist thing out there.

The people working there or attending it would be typecast as the next graduating class of Klansmen. White people do not look at black collages as the next graduating class of Black Panthers.

I really don't think a lot of white people sit around and talk or even think about it. I'm pretty sure at black collages, I would think anyway, that the classes being taught are pretty much the same as an open admissions collage would have? I've never been to either type of collage. But I don't think black only collages teach car-jacking "advanced class", or "crack 101", or "home burglary" also an advanced class.

I think reverse discrimination is one of the biggest problems between the races in this country today. I also don't think a white only collage would be teaching classes on "how to keep the black man down 101", or "modern day slavery- crack instead of chains" advanced class only, or "how to keep the Mexicans and black people fighting each other", also an advanced class.

Why is there a Miss Black America Pageant, but not a Miss White America Pageant? Why is there a Black Entertainment Television, but not a White Entertainment Television? Why is there a Black Congressional Caucasus, but not a White Congressional Caucasus? Why is there a NAACP, but not a NAAWP?

If you want to be treated the same, quit asking for special handouts because of your race. Quit acting like your different just because of your race, and almost everyone will quit trying to act like you are different just because of your race.

Nothing anyone can ever do will change the fact that you'll always have bad people in every race. We will always have niggers among Black people, you'll always white trash honkies among White people, and you'll always have greasy wetbacks among Mexicans. And I'm pretty much guessing that there will always be rude Europeans.

Believe it or not, white people know black people are black. I'm guessing black people know that white people are white. Short of being blind from birth, everyone pretty much knows what color they are, and what color everyone else is too. As I stated before, it's 2010 not 1963 in the Deep South, and its 2010 pretty much everywhere. I don't think slavery is a big problem in this country anymore. I also don't think anyone is alive today whose parents and most likely grandparents or even great-grandparents were even alive during the time in this country that slavery was allowed.

Here's another thing that should be made mandatory. Anyone receiving any type welfare, government housing, food stamps, and that type of government assistance should be made to pass a drug test before receiving any. Many businesses today make their employees take and pass drug test, and pass them many times and randomly. That means the people taking the test do not know when they will be made to take the test. If the people who go to work and pay taxes have to take and pass drug test in order to keep their jobs. Then I see no reason for the people who sit on their ass all day getting free money, free food, and a free place to live should not have to do the exact same thing in order to receive it.

There should also be a limit on how much and how often anyone could receive government assistance for.

# Chapter 6.

# States Rights.

One of the biggest problems with our Federal Government is that most people think it too big and too intrusive into our everyday rights and liberties. I agree totally. If the Federal Government would give some of the issues back to the states that created some of these problems we would all sleep better at night.

Take Roe vs. Wade for an example. I believe that was a case from the mid-west part of the country? Why should people in Georgia or Arizona care about whether an abortion is legal or illegal in Kansas or Missouri?

Abortion, gun-laws, speed-limits, seat-belt laws, drinking age, driver license age, criminal sentencing, age to be for marriage, gay marriage, tax rates, affirmative action, graduation test scores from all levels of schools. I am sure I missed a few more but I hope most all people can get my drift.

If Alabama decides to not use any affirmative action policies in their college admissions and just uses test scores and grades from high school transcripts that should be left up to Alabama. If Michigan wants to use affirmative action in deciding who gets to go to their school, then that's up to the voters in Michigan.

The Federal Government should not dictate to states how they run things like this. Believe me the voters who live in that state are perfectly capable of deciding these types of issues. The one big thing that piss's off people is when they have laws passed on them and they have no say so in the matter. That's so Un-American, which is why Ted Kennedy's old senate seat was lost to the Democrats. To many backroom secret meetings and midnight votes.

The only thing we Americans should allow in some of these laws would be some age limit restrictions. I don't think anyone has a problem with a minimum age being at least 18 before buying alcohol or smokes, voting, or marriage, or buying a gun.

If Florida wants to let an 18 year old (Legal Adult) buy beer in their state, then the people in Florida should make that decision not some Senator from Maine.

If Texas decides to let someone who has a felony conviction on their record own a gun again, after they complete whatever sentence was imposed on that person from that state. Then Texas should be able to make that decision, not some Senator from Vermont.

Here is another one, and I don't see what the big deal here is all about. Gay marriage, other than homosexuals who else should be concerned about this issue? If they want to get married…let them.

Make it legal just like a marriage between a man and a woman. And if they break up they have to get a divorce just like a man a woman. It would be a huge business, just think about it. Just like that, you've created a whole new business for lawyers. Gay divorce specialist lawyers. Make gay marriage legal and we could create thousands of new jobs. (This time no pun intended.)(OK there was a little pun intended)

The point I'm trying to make here is this, we don't need a Constitutional Amendment to deal with all of these things, at least not on a Federal level.

If Iowa wants to let 2 men marry each other or 2 women marry each other, why in the hell do people in Montana or Georgia care? If these 2 men or 2 women decide to move to a state that did not legalize marriage between same sex couples. Then under that state those 2 people are not married. If those 2 men or 2 women don't like it, then don't move there. I would suggest to those people who do get married, and then have to move and even for the ones who just want to move, is to keep an address in the state you got married in. That way you'll always be married in that state. For those of you say that's not fair, I don't care. Show me where it is written in your rights as an American citizen that life is supposed to be fair.

Hell, I don't care if other states decided to make all marriages that were not preformed in their state illegal. Back to the states rights thing again.

If California wanted to grant legal status there for workers or anyone really that would be their call. But they would also have to be responsible for them. If the then legal people in a certain state decide to leave that state without permission from the state that allowed them in and the state that they were wanting to go to. That would then make them illegal aliens. It would be then be up to the state that allowed them in. If they get arrested in Arizona, and they're not suppose to be there, then depending on how Arizona wanted to handle it. Either sending them back to California or back to their home country, or jail.

If they want to come here to this country, then they need to obey our laws. If they want to come here to this country, it is up to them to learn our laws, in our language, which is English. It should not be up to the USA to teach them our laws, or to even print them in 40 different languages. All the United States should do is to provide any country that asks us for a copy of our federal laws, and they can then ask each of the states for a copy of the laws in that state.

People, there are a lot of laws on the books that deal with illegal immigration. We need to enforce what we have now, and then see if we need to change any of them. If California let them come into their state, it would be like they would have a free travel range, and California's borders would be that range, or whatever area inside of California that they decided on. Anything outside of that would be breaking the law.

Education is something that should most definitely be left up to each state. Graduation test scores should be particular to each of the 50 states. All 50 states are different in so many ways, educations levels and abilities also.

I have no problem with the federal government sending out some guild lines, such as a student needs X amount of hours in school before they can receive a diploma, or even they need "X" amount of hours of Math, or English. But there does not need to be a test from the federal government taken before a student can graduate.

# Chapter 7.

# Social Security.

My next fix, Social Security. I wanted to do this here so that I can tie it into illegal immigration. First and foremost, if you were not born in this country, or born to legal parents you would not ever be able draw Social Security. I see that as a perk to Americans and Americans only. I could see making a few exemptions to this law. For example, if you worked legally in this country for say...25 years and could prove it. Then you would be able to draw an amount, but it could not exceed what you paid in.

Also, now here is the kicker, remember earlier when I said nothing is free, well that includes freedom.

Anyone who migrates to this country would be required to pay into Social Security but never draw from it. If you do not like that law, then don't come to America! Social Security just got healthy again.

Here's another good one, and I'll be coming back to the Congress and the Senate later as well as the other branches of our government later on. Did you know that the Congress and the Senate are not required to pay into Social Security? Also I'm guessing that the Executive Branch and the Supreme Court also do not pay in to it either. They have their own private retirement plan, and it's a whole lot better plan than Social Security, and we pay for that too.

When was the last time most of us were given the option of not having it already taken out of our paychecks? Did anyone outside of Washington D.C. know this matter has already been addressed?

The 28th Amendment to the Constitution states "Congress shall make no law that applies to the citizens of the United States that does not apply equally to the Senators or members of the House of Representatives, and Congress shall make no law that applies to the Senators and member of the House of Representatives that does not apply equally to the citizens of the United States." I'd have to say they've broke this one a few times.

Where's my diplomatic immunity? Where is my lifetime health care plan? When do I get to vote in my own pay raise? Where is my great retirement plan? Where is my free travel? Why can't I not pay Social Security taxes?

If insurance plans and retirement plans do better with more people in them, as we have always been told, then why is it that the entire country is not enrolled in the Government retirement and insurance plans?

Fixing Social Security like I have stated here would be the perfect fix, either political party could get it done. Who could possibly vote against giving older and or disabled American citizens a peace of mind for their long term retirement? And with our own money that we have already paid into the Social Security fund since we started working, mostly with very little or no say so. Social Security would be solvent forever.

Perhaps they could even take a little less each week out of our paychecks?

Now here I could see it being a good place to put a Constitutional Amendment making it impossible for the Government to do anything with these funds, other than for their intended purpose only. I would not do many Constitutional Amendments. But I think a few should be done to ease confusion on some issues. I would make burning the American flag in public or for public broadcast a jailable offence and a deportable offence if not both. Freedom of speech has nothing to do with burning our flag, that's just being an asshole.

My other one would be to make English the only official language of this country. Do you know how much money could be saved in this country by doing this one thing? Think about it, no longer would the federal government have to print things in many different languages, and the states would not have to do it either. I'd like to see Congress run that idea thru the accounting process to see just how much could be saved. I simply do not see it as being a problem for people who want to come to this country. They need to learn our language.

## Chapter 8.

# Crime

Crime, it's getting out of hand people. It's time to bring back true justice, and public executions. If you cut off a few hands for stealing on the town square, I can guarantee you that stealing will be cut down a great deal. Even if it's not cut down, most of it will not be done from repeat offenders. And no, you left-wing liberal extremist, I'm not talking about cutting of a 12 year olds hand because he stole a candy bar.

But I would be willing to cut off the hand of a 12 year old who has been caught red-handed breaking into someone's house or breaking into someone's car, for the umpteenth time.

Jail or prison should not be a badge of honor, and it is becoming just that for many young people. Prison is not a racial thing. It's a stupid, selfish, greedy, ignorant person thing. A lot of this has come from very poor parenting skills. Of course when kids are having kids what can you expect?

There is a huge difference between discipline and child abuse. Parents need to know the difference. Believe me I do know the difference, and yes, I've seen both.

Little Johnny and little Suzie are no different than little Tyrone and little Latoya. They both have 2 parents who are married, both have jobs, both live in the suburbs, both sets of kids are fairly good students.

Now we all know this seldom happens, so let's go to the real world for awhile. Tyrone and Latoya's dad was never in the picture, the mom works 2 jobs, and she tried hard to keep them together. But she always knew it wasn't going to happen, she's seen it to many times. She likes to going out on the weekend, she's human, has needs, and this crappy apartment sucks.

Tyrone got expelled from school 4 months ago for fighting and missing too many days of school. No big deal he has a pile of friends in the same boat. He's been arrested 2-3 times, but has always been released back to momma. Maybe a couple of times he had to spend a few hours in jail, that's no big deal, he just gets to brag to his buddies about it. After all he's only just turned 16. Well one Friday night, a couple of 40 ounces later, maybe a joint or 2, there are 4 of them hanging out, broke again. They decide they should have a car.

Of course Tyrone didn't know his home boy had that gun. Well things get out of hand, and they always do. The police come along at the worst possible moment, well for the thugs out robbing anyway. Just in time for the guy that just got car-jacked.

Another high speed case gets underway. Three wrecked cars later and a telephone pole down. Guess what, 2 out of the 4 got away. The one that brought the gun died in the wreck and poor Tyrone, he got busted up but not too bad. He was wearing the home boy's jacket, he gets charged with everything, including assault, gun, drugs, and car-jacking. He's looking at a 25 year sentence the hard way.

Oh by the way, little Johnny who just turned 17, just got his learners permit and made the baseball All-Star team, and his sister who is 16 and drinks like a fish and does Meth and Ecstasy just found out she is pregnant.

It's not about being white or black, sometimes kids just go bad. But when they do, make them take reasonability for their own actions. Tyrone needs to be charged as an adult, and is, but he cuts a deal and only gets 15 years, because he snitches out those 2 that got away.

Of course he pays dearly for that fact in prison. He makes parole after 8 years, he had to do at least half because of the gun. He's killed 10 months later during a robbery. Remember Suzie? Well she had the baby, got out of rehab, but still has that STD. But she cleaned up her act. Four years later got married and had 2 more kids, they are still married.

People, 2 parents make things a lot easier. Nothing is fool prove, you can have 10 parents and still have bad or mean kids, black or white or whatever.

People I have got no sympathy for any of them. Like I said before, this is the greatest country in the world today.

This is the only country that I know of that it doesn't matter to whom you were born to or to what status you were born into, you can become anything you want.....good or bad.

I think this is one of the biggest differences between the Democrats and the Republicans today. Most Republicans think, damn another thug out car-jacking, you should lock his ass up and throw away the key. Most Democrats think ohhhh that poor poor boy. The only reason he got into trouble was because he's black and poor, and can't get the education that rich white boys get.

Well they are both right and both wrong. I have got no problem with the second or even third chance, for some things, not all. He had his chance, a few times at the education and threw it away. He had a few chances before they threw him out of school. The color of his skin had nothing to do with it. If you make things like that a race issue, I don't care who you are, you're wrong.

I think a lot of black people should pay attention to what MLK Jr. really said. That one day, all people would be judged by the character of their deeds and actions instead of the color of their skin. Everything is not about the color of your skin, it's all about you. Back to page 1, its 2010 not 1963.

This takes us back to giving rights back to the individual states. If California wants their state prisoners to be able to sit around and watch T.V. that's fine by me. But if Georgia wants to work their state prisoners on a chain-gang, that should be up to Georgia.

Once you get rid of the riff-raff, gang-bangers, and outright criminals, this would help drive crime down. Bring back chain-gangs in prison, make them work their sentences off instead of sitting around watching cable television, lifting weights, and playing basketball. Do away with all those perks in prison.

You're never going to get rid of all crime, that's never going happen anywhere I don't think. But if the punishment for committing a crime is a plush resort with more amenities than most of the people in there ever had before they went to prison. That's not much of a deterrent for people to stop committing crimes.

One more thing make cocaine and crack have pretty much the same jail time in sentencing people. And you have got to stop these white collar crimes, corporate crimes and fraud and schemes. Do you know how hard it is to justify giving Tyrone a 15 year sentence at 17 years old?

Then you see 3 corporate types (all white) put their trial off for 6 years, while they remain out on bond, flying in on their private jets for another motion to post-pone their trial date again.

By doing that you give the news people and the Democrats ammunition to shoot back at you. You know they are out there spending all that money they stole, and living large and laughing the whole time. If you had enough to charge them with a crime, then you had enough to take it to court.

Make the punishment fit the crime. I keep hearing how the police are always saying, well….. we just arrest them, and you'll have to talk to the judge about how come they were back on the streets. Fine, let's talk about that subject. It's real simple and it will solve another racial issue at the same time.

Now I understand each person and each case is different. But if you had set in stone guild lines about certain offences, such as any person caught with pot possession under say 1 ounce, their first time would be 2 years probation and 100 hours of community service, and maybe a small fine.

Second time would be 6 months in the county jail followed by 3 years probation, and a bigger fine. Third offence would be 2 years in state prison, and they have to serve it all. For armed robbery of anything, first offence is 5 years state prison, if the gun was used at all make it 10 years.

You can work on the numbers any way you want to, that would be up to each state. But you take race totally out of the picture.

Homeowners should never be arrested for shooting someone that is trying to break into their house, or trying to steal anything from their property. In fact shoot them if they are trying to break into or steal anything on their property.

That's how you cut down on crime. Just make sure you are right. Just remember anything worth shooting, is worth shooting twice.

# Chapter 9.

# Creating Jobs.

Well, let see......what shall I tackle next? Creating jobs in this country for American citizens.

All jobs in the U.S.A. would be given to Americans first. If no legal American wanted that particular job, then it could be given to legal aliens. I think anyone out there would be very hard pressed to name one job in this country, which cannot be done from someone that's already legally here in this country.

I do not know of any particular job in this country that cannot be done by people already here. Yes the cost for some things might go up, but then again so would some wages. At least they would be paying taxes to this country instead of sending their money to another country.

I'm guessing most people have not been to other countries to work? Almost all other countries have Visas and work permits, and they have limits to them. Most work visas for other countries are only good for certain periods of time. There is a reason for that, it keeps jobs in that country, for people from that country. I really don't think we need thousands and thousands of doctors from India. I also do not think the only people who can pick fruit or produce need to come from Mexico.

As I said before, we here in America make almost nothing anymore. That's a damn shame too. We were once the biggest exporter of..... EVERYTHING.

Now we import pencils, blue jeans, frozen fish, dildos, dishes, socks, microwave ovens, televisions, light bulbs, and hell we can't even build our own cars in our own country anymore. Why do we need cars to be assembled partly in Mexico and Canada? This may well piss off a lot of people, but I really don't care. The main reason most of these jobs left our country is because of the unions.

I'm all for a fair wage for a fair days work. The unions were a good things many many years ago. But in today's world and with how things are today in general, they hurt a lot more than they help. No, I have never been a member of a union, nor would I become one.

I have managed several union companies on jobs that I have been on. So yes, I have been around them a lot. I have worked around union members and union companies for years, but not once have I ever been asked if I would consider joining them.

I've seen the good and the very bad. My father was a union worker, but back then they took pride in being a union worker.

They were paid better than non-union workers, and they had earned it I believe. Today, it is no longer about the quality of the work that they perform. It is about, how can they screw the current client out of more money and get more people hired on. It's about how they can prolong the job so that it will last longer and they can keep working there longer.

I've seen union jobs that have put people on the job just to screw things up. That way more people had to be hired just to fix their own screw ups. I've seen union jobs tell newly hired workers to slow down. They didn't want them to do any more work than was absolutely needed for that day or that shift. If they did more than what was required they would in turn make the other union workers look bad.

These are the very same unions who back these Democrats in Congress. Yes, that has a lot to do with me disliking Democrats. I've seen it happen too many times, the unions are just like the Democrats, and they don't care about their members either. The Democrats just want that vote, and the unions just want their dues.

I've seen people who have never worked a day in their life for any union go to a union hiring hall and pay the Business Agent money under the table and buy their union card just to get on a job.

These days all the unions cares about are getting their dues from the working people.

No not all of the union companies out there are bad. Neither are all of the union member's bad workers. I have been on jobs that had union companies on them, and they did good work. But, the bigger that the jobs are that do have union companies on them, the worse they become. I've seen jobs where both union and non-union companies were on, and I've seen the union go out of their way to steal things, and vandalize work that has already been completed from the non-union companies, just trying to make them look bad.

I knew a helper. He had just turned 19 years old, on a job (he was non-union) that had both working on that job, union and non union. He told me one day that about 10 union guys had him cornered in the elevator and asked him why he was working for a rat (rat is what the union people call non-union people) contractor. He told them that this was his first job ever and he was just happy to have a job. He said they talked trash about the company he worked for and how non-union companies were the scum of the earth. After work he told me, he thought how funny it seemed to him. A brand new construction worker like him someone who didn't know anything about either union or non union work or companies.

That the one thing they never said to him was, why don't you join a union company? They never once said anything good about their own company or their own union.

All they had to say was how bad working for a non-union company was. They only had bad things to say about the other side of the coin, but nothing good to say about their own side of the coin.

Does that remind you of anything? Such as Democrats saying how bad the Republicans are, but never saying anything good about their own. I firmly believe that is the reason the Democrats lost the election in 2004. All they ever said was how bad George W Bush was. They never once said our guy Kerry, is better than your guy, just that your guy was awful.

Back to jobs, sorry I get on a rant sometimes and just can't let it go.

This is where the federal government can and should come into play. Make imports have the same type of restrictions that our exports have. If another country subsidizes a company in their country that makes steel and wants to import it into our country. Make a tax on it so that it cost as much or cost more to import it into our country so our companies are not at a disadvantage. But we also have to keep the price of the steel that we do make here affordable.

The unions here have made the price of doing business here extremely high. There is no way the cost of making a steel beam here should be 3-4 times higher than an imported steel beam.

We don't need to subsidize a company here to make less. We don't need to pay farmers to not grow things. We need more farmers growing more things. Free market will dictate price controls. All of these people out of work will go to work, if there are jobs out there for them.

If a car company wants to sell their cars here in our country, then we say fine sell your cars here. But if you want to sell 100,000 cars here then you have to let us sell 100,000 cars in your country.

If you put a tariff on our product we're going to put a bigger tariff on yours. Why should it cost 40,000 dollars to buy a Ford in Japan that sells for 20,000 here?

If Toyota decides if they build a car plant in our country and that it can save money by making them here instead of shipping them here, that's fine. Why can't Dodge build a plant there, and save the same amount of money, after all it's the same distance from California to Japan as it from Japan to California? If Dodge decides it wants to sell cars there and does not want to build a plant there, then yes it might cost more to build them here and then ship it to Japan.

But there should not be outrageous tariffs deciding how much things should cost.

Common sense needs to be put back in practice and used more often in business decisions. As long as the unions keep driving up health care cost, wages, and other benefits this country will never be able to survive in a global environment.

I know in today's world, if I owned a company and I made blue jeans. My blue jeans were as good as any other jeans on the market. But my cost to make 1 pair of jeans in this country was 20 dollars. The market dictates that my jeans sell for 22 dollars a pair, to say someone like Wal-Mart.

But after I pay for the employees wage, health care, retirement, vacation, sick days, and a ton of other things just to keep them happy and not to go on strike. I then get to pay for the material to make the jeans, light bills, rent on the building, lawyers, advertising to sell the jeans, stock holder dividends, office staff, office equipment, a payroll company, equipment to make the jeans, up keep on all of the equipment, and a ton of other stuff. Yes I too would like to make a profit. After all I started the company to make money.

But here lies the problem, my main competitor, blue jean company number 2 decided that they can close up shop here and move the whole factory to Mexico. They can make basically the same pair of jeans that I make, but their cost per pair will now be only 6 dollars. After 2 years, they will have paid for the move and will be making 16 dollars per pair profit. But with me, the union has already told me in the next 2 years they will want a 10% raise, and 2 more vacations days, plus a ton of other things.

My point is this, this is why companies have left our country. That is where all the jobs have gone to and why. If I owned a company here and this played out this way, I see 2 options for the owner, one, move overseas, or two, close up shop.

## Chapter 10.

# If I were the President.

Crime is down. Social Security is projected to be on the good side of the ledger forever now. Which means we can now give senior citizens a real annual raise? There are hardly any illegal aliens left, and Wall Street is up. Since the stock market is doing so well these days, that means there are plenty of jobs and people are working. The more people working means more tax money for Uncle Sam. Ahhh a strong Uncle Sam, now the military can get a raise.

Oh by the way, I reinstated the draft, mandatory 2 years service, with a military option for the third year, and a mutual option for the fourth, fifth, and sixth year. If nothing else these young people will learn something for 2 years, even if it is learning how to break big rocks into little rocks.

I honestly think I could have this country back to where it should be in about 5-7 years. I think I could have the whole deficit gone, and be operating smoothly in that time frame. There are many problems in this country, with that I agree whole heartedly, but I think we make more out of them for the most part then is really needed.

That's because the politicians need something to talk about and to help keep people distracted from real problems in this country. Don't you just love how all of the big issues come up right before the elections, but they never have a vote on big items right before the elections.

I would make it mandatory that all items that have been debated on all thru the year in congress, would have to be voted on no later than 2 weeks before the November elections. That would keep things fresh in the voters mind. It would be pretty tough on a Senator running for re-election, to have to explain why that 2 weeks ago he voted to cut the cost of living raise for Social Security.

Or explain why he raised payroll taxes for people making between 30,000 and 150,000 dollars a year, but not for people making over 150,000 a year. Then he has to also explain why he voted to give himself a 12% raise. Do all of this right before an election it will keep the PR firms out of the business of government. When that Senator has to explain things to the people who voted him into office, instead of spending millions of dollars bashing is opponent in the upcoming election. Then perhaps this country can get back to running a government for the people, by the people.

I don't see this happening because at the present I'm not really planning on running for president.

I also do not see anyone from any political party ready to stand up and do what is needed to do to get this country back on track. I also do not think that there is a George Washington or Thomas Jefferson out there. My only hope is that they are out there, and they just don't know it yet.

But if I were the President of the United States of America, things would get done that need to get done in this country. I think the Greatest generation of people in this country were the George Washington's, Thomas Jefferson's, and the Ben Franklin's. Everything they did, they did without any backup.

They did it all with common sense, guts, and they had a purpose. The next greatest generation, I think was the one that fought in WW II. They fought for their country, and they used common sense, guts, and they too had a purpose.

If this country is going to make a comeback, and become what it once was, a great country. It will have to happen in the next 20 years or it will never happen again. If it doesn't happen by then I believe it will be too late to change course. If it does happen, they will in turn become the third greatest generation this country has ever known.

This country needs a leader or leaders who can and will lead and unite. At present we have none, Democrat or Republican, or any other party.

If I were the President, the first thing I would do after being sworn in to protect this country from all enemies foreign and domestic. I would have both branches of Congress arrested. I would then suspend the Supreme Court. I would bring in the military leaders from all of the branches and remind them that they work for me. I would suspend the Constitution, with the support of the military. I would basically create a military coup.

I think at this point in time in history they are the only ones that can make a real difference in this country.

This may seem like a third world option, but there is no other way. The party in power, whoever it may be, controls too much power. They control the press, the military, secret service, ATF, FBI, and a whole host of other police type agencies. If anyone would dare suggest this course of action, they would be branded as loonies, crackpots, and extremist, and be at the very least arrested. Most likely they would die from something like suicide, the kind where their hands are tied behind their backs and they shoot themselves 5 times.

Read The Declaration of Independence, it requires us to do these things. We as citizens of this country have an obligation to the rest of this country. If the government will not listen to the will of the people, then the people are supposed to get rid of that government and start over. Instead we keep electing the same ol' assholes, or at the very least, the same type assholes to keep screwing us over.

The only way to get our current cycle of government out of power is by a military coup. I see no other way. I'm not talking about some 2 bit dictatorship like in Cuba or North Korea. The military would simply take control to keep order.

Believe it or not, I do believe that is why the second amendment was placed in the Constitution. The right to keep and bear arms, back when it was written everyone had a weapon. It was meant I think, to provide a way for regular citizens to help protect their families, their land, put food on the table, and to help protect their country. Not all enemies come from outside of our borders. That's why part of the oath of office says from all enemies' foreign and domestic.

Washington D.C. would be gone as we know it today. There would be a new focus and a new purpose for people in the government.

They would need to realize that their function at work would be for the greater good of the country, not what they might be able to get out of it.

States would be able to keep a lot more of the taxes that they collect. It would be used for things in that state. I do not think people in Texas want to pay for snow removal in Minnesota. I also do not think people in Montana want to pay for hurricane damage in Louisiana. States would still pay their fair share of taxes to the federal government. The federal government would still provide a lot of the same services it provides today, to some extent. I think people in each state should have a lot of the say-so about how their taxes are spent.

I do not want a Congressman from New York City deciding that I need to be 21 before I can buy a beer. Or a Senator from Nevada deciding that I need to pay a higher tax on a pack of cigarettes. I'm from Georgia, if Georgia decides that 25 is the legal drinking age, then so be it. If Georgia decides that they want to put a 5 dollar tax on every pack of cigarettes, that's fine too. If I smoke and I do not want to pay that much for a pack, I'll go somewhere else to buy them.

Common sense, the people need to use it or they'll lose it. Because that is what is happening in this country today. Bigger government is not the right answer. It's not even close.

Our government wastes so much money each day it's not even funny anymore. I saw an article the other day, which to me typified our current government. It was a comment from a person about an article on government spending. A person had said they need to cut out most foreign aid and pork-barrel politics. And the response back from a Senator was that foreign aid and pork projects inserted into spending bills really didn't account for that much of our debt. That is how far out of touch our government is today with the citizens of this country. If it accounts for any of it, it's too much.

If you go to the grocery store and you have only a certain amount of money, and you get to the check-out stand and find out you don't have enough money to pay for everything you want. You'll have to put something back that you wanted. Are you going to put back the medicine that your child needs, or are you going to put back that 12 pack of beer? The working citizens of this country know the correct answer. The politicians only know the correct answer at election time. At no time should our government ever be allowed to have a debt.

Common sense again people, if you can't afford it, you don't get it. If people were in debt by as much as our country is today, about 5-6 times the amount of money they take in each year. We would not be able to get enough credit to buy a pack of gum. But since the Fed is run by the Federal Government they can still give themselves the best AAA credit rating, and/or they just print more money. That must be nice, if you run out of money just print more of it.

The government needs to be run like a business. The president as CEO and the vice president as CFO. You either break even or turn a profit or we will get someone in there that can.

I don't even have a problem with the federal government collecting a little more than is needed. I have no problem with them having a surplus. The states would and should go to the federal government to borrow money from if they had to. But then only in times of emergencies or some kind of very special need.

Since we as a country would be starting over on a lot of things, I think we as citizens should be given some of the same breaks our states and the federal government would be getting. I would give every US legal citizen the option of having their entire credit rating totally washed clean. It would be a one shot deal, no do over's, no wipe some but leave some.

It would be all or nothing. I would then put all credit rating companies under control of the federal government. No three or four companies should have that much control over people's lives. That used to be called a monopoly, and they were broken up for the good of the people.

I would have it set up so that the vice-president actually had a job to do again. My new system would make it that both the President and the Vice President would have a very specific task. One would be in charge of the domestic policies and the other in charge of foreign policies. I might have to keep a few of the Ambassadors around in order to keep foreign affairs in order, at least for awhile.

I would assure world leaders around the world that this is only a temporary position in this country, and after the new elections, and the new Congress and courts were sworn in that our Constitution would be reapplied.

I would also change a few of our election laws. I have never understood why if the President is the most powerful person in government, why do Senators get elected to 6 year terms and the President only gets 4 years? I would cut out all of those lifetime perks they get now. All of Congress would go to a 2 year election cycle. I might let the Senators go to a 4 year cycle. I would then change the presidents to a 5 or maybe 6 year term.

There would be a 2 maybe 3 term limit on both houses of Congress. If a state had someone who they thought was doing a great job as a Congressman, and their 2 term limit was up, then that person could run as a Senator. Or they could wait a term out of office then run again. That great job that they thought he was doing might not look so good after someone else was doing it for a couple of years. They could also forget about that part time schedule that they follow now. It would turn into a real job.

All political meeting in both houses of Congress would be broadcast to the public at all times. After all they are public servants.

Once something was agreed upon, it would have to be posted in print and the internet for at least 1 week before a vote could be convened. There would not be any midnight laws passed in this country. Anything signed into law would have to be open and aboveboard. The only exception to this would/could be matters of national security. Believe it or not there are some things that people are better off not knowing. If the military and the president decide that someone should be assassinated for the good of the country or the good of the world then most people do not need to know about that.

If the military and the president decide that certain people or groups of people need to be monitored, that is not information that is needed to be debated on C-Span.

I have no problem profiling certain groups of people. If Muslims want to come into this country I have no problem putting them thru extra security procedures first. I for one think they have earned it. If they don't like it, then don't come here. I'm sure there are some good Muslims in the world. Most groups of people that would fall under this type of scrutiny would not want to be associated with the bad people in their own groups.

If the people are not doing anything wrong they will have nothing to be worried about.

My next task would be to outlaw political parties. A person would have to run on their own merits. No one person has all the same ideas and believes as another person, (unless you're a Democrat today) why should they run under the same banner? I would make it a law both houses of Congress would have to go back to their home states and have a state wide vote on any federal law that is proposed in Washington D.C. They in turn would have to vote how their home state voted. The people in those states are the ones that sent them to Congress in the first place.

The politicians should be doing what people in their home states want done. I believe that would put an end to back-room deals in Congress.

I would then summon all 50 Governors to my office and tell them to hold new elections. In the new elections I would suggest that no one that has ever held an office in Washington D.C. should be allowed to be elected. Maybe if the new politicians coming to Washington D.C. didn't already know how to lie and cheat the tax payers, maybe they could get something done. I would tell the governors that the states were going to start being more responsible for things in their own state.

I would have a list of things that they would need to put on their state ballot. Things such as abortion, gun control, drinking age, speed limits, illegal immigrates to some extent, and a whole host of other things that the federal government was no longer going to decide for them.

Governors of states and people elected to state Supreme Courts would become important people, and it would become a very powerful job again. I would strongly recommend to each state that they need to set term limits on state office. I think 2 terms are enough for any office.

Why is there a federal law stating that the President can only hold office for a maximum of two four year terms, but Congressmen and Senators can hold the same job for as long as they can get elected? Also why is it that the Supreme Court has a lifetime appointment? I thought all 3 branches of government were supposed to be equal?

If the military or the post office makes people retire at 65, I think all government work should fall under that guide line, or none of them. I would not put age limits on all 3 branches of government.

But I also do not think someone who is in their 70's, 80's or even their 90's and have been in office for 20-40 years need to be there any longer. I have no problem with someone who is 70 or 80 or even 90 running for office. I do believe older people have a tremendous amount to offer. For most people the older they get, the wiser they get. But term limits would put an end to a lot of Washington D.C. crap.

I would also do away with the law only allowing the president to hold office for two four year terms. They could only be elected to 2 terms in a row, but after being out of office for a full term, 4 years they could run again, and if elected they could then run for their second term.

It would be the same way for all 3 branches of government. I do not think any term for any office should go past 4 years.

For the Supreme Court, since it cannot be a job that someone is elected to. I would make their appointments for a set amount of time. I think a term of 10 years would be fine. Either that or make it for 2 terms maximum in a row, with each term to be five years. That way if they tried passing stupid laws, they could be dismissed after 5 years. In order for them to be dismissed after their first term, both houses of Congress would have to vote on it. If there were a tie, then the President would decide.

In fact at anytime both houses of Congress could decide to hold a vote to decide if a Supreme Court justice could be removed from the bench. But only if the President calls for the vote. Remember there are 3 branches of the government. The same rules would apply for that vote, just like it does with the Supreme Court now, a simple majority. If both houses of Congress wanted to call for a vote to remove a justice from the bench without Presidential approval, that would be allowed also. But it would take at least 60% of both houses to pass.

Now for the good part, what's good for one branch of government is good for the others also.

If the Supreme Court decided they wanted to remove a member of either house of Congress, then they could hold a vote also. The same rules apply here as before. If they decide to do it at the Presidents urging, then a simple 5-4 majority will do. If they decide to do it without Presidential approval then they would need a 7-2 vote.

If either leader of either house of Congress, or the Chief Justice of the Supreme Court decided to call for a vote to remove the President from office they could as well. All three of those people together could call for a full vote to remove the President from office. As with the other branches of government, a simple majority would be enough.

If all 3 leaders did not agree, but 2 out of the 3 did, then they could still call for a vote, but would need 60% to remove the President from office. One out of the three would not be able to call for a vote. That would be too easy, and every time someone got pissed off at someone else they would be calling for a vote.

Lobbying would and should be illegal to or for any member elected to any government office in the United States. Also this would apply to all members of all city, county, state, and federal government. Lobbying is legalized bribery.

Here's another novel idea, I would make the different departments of the government actually work together for a common purpose, like the FBI, CIA, NSA. I would also do away with a few of the Federal departments I'm guessing. Every member of every branch of the government would be required to pay all taxes just like everyone else was. They would have no special retirement accounts or health care plans.

Fraud would be handled quickly and harshly in areas like Medicare, Welfare, SEC, the FED banking, and many other areas. There would not be any more 500 dollar hammers or 3000 dollar toilet seats.

I would make it mandatory that in order to draw welfare check, the person had to pass a drug test first. There would be a lot of new laws regarding the welfare system, such as time limits on how long they could draw for.

Some of the things that I would purpose would not be popular to some people, but I think most people would be for the changes. Most all taxpaying citizens I believe would love most of them.

At no time in history have all of the people in any country all been happy at the same time. That's because all people are different, just like countries are different.

# Chapter 11.

# Foreign Policy.

The foreign policies of this country have pretty much sucked for years. This next statement is not meant to be a slur against our military at all. But we have not fought a real war since the end of World War 2. I believe it started with President Truman in Korea. General Sherman said it best, war is hell.

I simply do not think you can fight a war between countries with a lot of rules. In Vietnam we were not allowed to cross rivers, but they could. We were not allowed to fly over certain places but they could. We were not allowed to bomb certain places, so they just put things that they didn't want bombed around those places. That's not fighting a war. I do not think our military has ever started a war. Wars are started by stupid politicians, not soldiers. Soldiers simply have to fight and die in them. Those same politicians stay at home, all nice and cozy, not out in the rain and snow and heat.

And what the hell is up with the United States arguing with Japan for over Okinawa? Didn't we kick their ass and take that island? In my book that makes it ours, not theirs.

You do not fight a war to not lose it, or to be concerned about civilian deaths. You do not fight a war for CNN. You do not fight a war for oil, wood, gold, or any other materials. You fight a war with another country to win, period. You go to war with another country when there is no other way to resolve whatever your differences are. The oil, gold, wood, water, or whatever other natural resources they have goes to the winner. After the war is over, we're also not going to be giving land back that we fought and died for.

Take the first Gulf War for example, if that had been me in charge of our forces, after we kicked Iraq's ass. I would have installed an oil pump on the coast and started pumping oil. I would have put 1 in Kuwait, 1 in Saudi Arabia, and 1 in Iraq. We went to that war because one well armed country decided to take over another country and their resources. We went there because there was a lot concern Iraq might also invade Saudi Arabia. We set up camp there so that Iraq would not invade them too.

So after everything was said and done, we have helped keep Iraq out of Saudi Arabia and also gave Kuwait back to the rightful people who should be running that country.

If every country on the planet is going to call us every time that something like this happens, fine call us. We will come and bail your ass out of the bind that your country happens to be in. But know this before you call us, we will be sending you a bill for services rendered. If they don't like that deal, then call someone else. Or they can deal with whatever the problem is on your own. Kuwait could have been spending billions and billions of dollars designing and building their own military hardware, but they did not. Yes they had some things, mostly purchased from us. But with hindsight being 20/20, I guess they didn't have near enough.

I see no reason why we should not be compensated for having all of the tools needed to do the job. We took the time and money and effort to design and build what we need, why can't other countries do the same.

The U.N. is a joke. There are five countries with an all powerful veto vote. If one of the five doesn't like something they can just say no, and all action stops. If they want us to play the role of the world policeman, that's fine. But they will need to pay for the United States to play world policeman.

You may have to pay us in money, oil, land, or whatever you have to pay with. Take Kuwait as an example, they were invaded, their country was looted.

Maybe they didn't have money to pay. We should have set up a couple of oil wells and we would pump say, 2 million barrels of oil a day for 10 years. We do the same thing in Iraq, but we pump 2 million barrels of oil a day for 25 years. For Saudi Arabia we get to buy their oil at half price for 10 years. Remember nothing is free. Freedom is not free and war certainly is not free either.

When it comes to the United States going to another country to help them in their time of need, there would be a few other changes I would make also.

I firmly believe that under only one circumstance would any American service personnel be allowed to be put on trial in that country for something that they did there. That one circumstance would be if the United States decided to let it happen. First of all we would convene a military court to decide the what's, and where's and when's and if any charges were warranted to proceed with. If it turned out that we thought someone had did something bad enough to be brought up on charges then we would handle it.

Our military leaders are perfectly capable of policing our own people. The reason behind this is simple.

If we were not there protecting some other countries ass, the problem would not have happened in the first place. This is not to say our soldiers could do whatever they wanted to do either. Things like rape, out right murder, looting, and things along that nature would have swift and severe penalties.

I would direct the military to not waste a lot of time on investigations of who shot who in an apartment building, and if any of the people shot were civilians or militants. If they were in the building and shooting at our troops then they are the bad guys too. I am so tired of hearing about how we killed innocent civilians.

If they let some militant sit in the middle of their house or school or church, then they are just as guilty as the person doing the shooting.

I stated earlier that as the President I would be giving the states back a lot of rights that the federal government has taken over. I would tell some of these countries that they need to start looking out for their own interest also.

As I stated very early on, I am not a well educated person. But I cannot see how us giving other countries aid, does anything for us? I honestly believe that right after they cash our check, they start laughing at us, again.

A lot of people would have to make one hell of a case in order to receive foreign aid from me. How much foreign aid do we receive from other countries?

The drug countries could simply forget about getting any type of aid. It's been 25 maybe 35 years that we have been fighting the war on drugs? I believe I'll go ahead and call that one a loss. Come on people, we can put a man on the moon and watch it on TV. We can dive machines with video cameras to the deepest parts of the oceans. We have satellites many hundreds of miles in space that can read the date a dime was made. But we can't spot 5 tons of cocaine under a bunch of bananas?

No I do not think legalizing the possession of illegal drugs is the right way to go either. The marijuana and cocaine and heroin and all of the other ones that are out there today need to be kept as illegal and kept out of the country to start with. Marijuana is a lot tougher than the others to keep out, it can be grown here. But there again, I would leave things like that to the states.

If a state decided to make marijuana legal in their state. That would be up to the voters. If Florida wanted to make the possession of marijuana up to two ounce legal then after the whole state voted and approved it, then they could.

If Tennessee decided to make the possession of any marijuana a jailable offence, then I'd suggest you didn't drive thru Tennessee on your way to Florida. It would be like everything else in life, very taxable.

I did not realize the purpose of NAFTA was for us to export jobs to Mexico, and for Mexico to export illegal drugs to us, because that's about all it's been able to do so far.

China, jeez what a joke that has turned out to be. I do not think everyone else in the world is wrong about their currency being undervalued. I've seen too much from too many other countries also, not just the US.

This is simple, it they will not adjust it correctly then the rest of the world should do it for them.

By that I mean if they hold bonds and treasury notes worth 3 trillion dollars and after careful calculations and adjustments we determine that the 3 trillion we owe should only be 1 trillion, then we only owe 1 trillion. If you put a situation like that on the bargaining table, then people and countries will pay attention. Of course there is always another alternative out there. We simply tell them to adjust it or we will no longer trade anything with you. I'm fairly sure Japan or South Korea would be willing to pick up any slack in television sells, and stuffed animals.

What do really get from there that we can't get somewhere else, or make here?

Now for the clown countries, we will always have them, we always have. The places like Cuba, North Korea, Iran, and I'm sure there are a few more out there. We will also always have the Napoleons of the world, the Castro's, and that idiot from Iran, and that Chavez guy from some little rinky dinky country in South America. Those people who run their countries are like a mad 8 year old child who was spoiled. They want to take their ball and go home if they don't get their way. Either spank them and send them home, or ignore them.

They're going to talk and squawk no matter what we do or say anyway. So why lose any sleep over them, we just keep a close eye on them to make sure they don't get overly stupid. (Well….no more stupid than normal.)

Here's another thing that I do not agree with as far as our foreign policy. I do not think we should be sticking our noses in the way other countries in the world do things in their country. We'll use Chine again as an example. The big thing with them is their record on human rights. I don't really care how they treat their citizens. I just don't care, if it does not affect me or my country.

But I also don't care if some people here want to support their dissidents. But as a country we should not be involved.

If they want to treat their own citizens like crap, then it's up to their own citizens to do something about it, not ours. If we think it so bad, then we need to stop having anything to do with that country. That means no trading anything with that country. If we as a country have a problem with another country, then we as a country should take that problem up with them. If we can't get the problem resolved diplomatically, but as a country we feel that we can't abide whatever the problem is. Then we need to cut our ties to that country. Why act like a hypocrite about it?

If we don't like Chinas treatment of their own citizens, then why do we even trade with them? I can't see how us having it both ways is going to help their citizens either. After all it is our trading with them that keeps their citizens working. Perhaps if their people were not working so much, maybe they could find time to change their own country.

We need to stop trying to shove our way of life, and our religious beliefs, and our political system down other countries throats. None of which are perfect by the way.

Hell we can't even agree in our own country about most things. A landslide election in our country anymore is 53% to 47%. That's not a landslide, that complete apathy for the political system that we have in place. I want to see a presidential election in this country where someone wins 75% to 25%. That's a person the whole country can rally around, and be proud of. Most of our elections nowadays, the losing side just sits around and bitchs and moans for a year or so.

# Chapter 12.

# Ramblings and Rants.

I have made this statement many times, and will continue to make it, Fox News is very 1 sided in their point of views. To me the only news media outlet on any of the other stations that are more one sided in their opinions than Fox News, is all of the rest of them. To me, I think it is a damn shame only 1 station in the entire nation has the guts to stand up to Washington D.C. and to the Democrats.

Like I said they are very 1 sided in their point of view, it just happens to be the truth, and right, most times. No one is right all of the time.

The Democrats have put a person in the White House that if the real truth ever comes out, most likely should never have been allowed to run for President in the first place. I would retract this statement if I'm proven wrong and all of the questions would be answered publicly about his passport and overseas traveling when he was younger. Also questions about his parent's residency requirements, and their travel outside of this country.

I, as a working American taxpayer have many problems with our current president and politics in general.

The current President who after being elected now all of a sudden knows how to create jobs in this country. This is from a person who has never held a real job in his life which was not somehow backed by the government. (Taxpayer money) He is going to tell Wall Street how businesses should be ran, and this is from a person who has never run a business. This is a person who is going to improve the whole education system, all from a person who hides his own collage records. This is a person who condemns cheating and dishonesty, this is from the person who's known associates have criminal records. We're not even going to bring Chicago politics or his preacher into the picture.

This is a person who says the rest of America needs to learn from his religion, even as he mocks the Christian faith and says this is not a Christian country any longer. This is a person who says he promotes openness and wants his presidency to be the most transparent ever. This is from the person who hides his birth certificate, and doesn't let C-Span televise congressional bills that he wants to get passed. This is the person who has late night meetings with union leaders, and members of his own political party to try and figure out ways to pass bills in secret. This is a person who embraces and bows down to people and countries that have attacked and mocked this country. This is from our military leader.

This is a person who says he respects our American Heritage. Yet, I and many believe he is dedicated to making Socialism the mainstream here.

Many people may not agree with this statement, but on paper I believe the most asinine political system ever devised is the Communist/Socialist system. There are only a few small problems with it. The main one being is that it will never work. It is designed to fail, even if it was run perfectly. No political system is or ever will be run perfectly.

If anyone has any ambition, the system will fail. If anyone wants to think for themselves, the system will fail.

If anyone thinks the government is not all smart and knows what is best for them, then the system will fail. If anyone thinks that working harder should get them ahead, then the system will fail. If anyone thinks saving money for a rainy day is a good idea, then the system will fail. The Communist/Socialist system is a total failure in its own makeup. The Communist/Socialist system basically states that everyone works for the common good of the country, and that no one owns anything, but that everyone owns everything. So what do they do next, they put someone in charge of it. Of course he has more than other people. They have just set someone up to be better than others and to have more than others.

But by doing that, you have just defeated the entire Communist/Socialism system.

Communist/Socialism is and always will be bound to fail, and as Margret Thatcher once said "The problem with socialism is that you eventually run out of other peoples' money." As Thomas Jefferson once said, "A government big enough to give you everything you want, is big enough to take everything you have." Here's another one from Thomas Jefferson "The democracy will cease to exist when you take away from those who are willing to work and give to those who would not."

Those founding fathers were pretty smart back then to come up with quotes that still apply in today's world. That was way before the Communist/Socialist systems were even thought about. That applied 250 years ago, and they apply today. They were pretty smart 30 years ago too. I'm not real sure about the people in government today.

Just think about the founding fathers 250 odd years ago, they didn't even have the internet, laptops, cell phones, GPS, or even spell-check. I wonder how they did all that stuff, you know........ like creating a country? Do you think maybe they had to think for themselves? Maybe they even used .......heaven forbid......common sense. That's something that is in very short supply these days.

There once was a pamphlet that came out monthly called Common Sense. Now-a-days we have blogs, and face book. Things where people get to say whatever they want to say, without having to say something to someone's face.

I wonder what George Washington's face book would have said about being the first President? I wonder how Paul Revere ever found his way at night on horseback, without a GPS? I wonder if Ben Franklin would have goggled diplomacy in the mid 1700's? I wonder if Thomas Jefferson would have looked up, how to write a Declaration of Independence on the internet .......before writing The Declaration of Independence?

I've read a few articles about Democracies, and most people/experts say that a true Democracy can only last for around 200-300 years, before it implodes. That's only if it is run correctly. About the time our original thirteen states adopted their new Constitution in 1787, Alexander Tyler, a Scottish history professor at the University of Edinburgh, had this to say about the fall of the Athenian Republic some 2,000 years earlier:

"A Democracy is always temporary in nature; it simply cannot exist as a permanent form of government."

"A Democracy will continue to exist up until the time that voters discover they can vote themselves generous gifts from the public treasury."

"From that moment on, the majority always vote for the candidates who promise the most benefits from the public treasury, with the result that every Democracy will finally collapse due to loose fiscal policy, which is always followed by a dictatorship."

It is said that there are a number of different stages to a Democracy.

1st. From bondage to spiritual faith.

2nd. From spiritual faith to great courage.

3rd. From great courage to liberty.

4th. From liberty to abundance.

5th. From abundance to complacency.

6th. From complacency to apathy.

7th. From apathy to dependence.

8th. From dependence back into bondage.

As a country, I think we are split at this point in time with 25% of the people at stage 5, and 50% of the people at stage 6, and 25% of the people at stage 7.

At the rate we are going in this country right now, we will be lucky to hit the high mark of 300 years. No country in the history of this planet has ever had a perfect political system. No country has ever had a military force that was never defeated in battle. No country has ever had a perfect history. We will not be the exception.

A Democracy will start to fall apart when the people in charge of it try to appease all of the people in it at the same time. I think the next 2 elections in this country will be its last defining moment. If this country goes the way of the last election, we will only speed up the end of the United States of America. Once that happens we will be another Europe here. I foresee about 4 maybe 5 small countries here.

The weakest and the first that will fall will be the northeast states, we'll call that country....New France....after all they're already rude anyway. Maine, Vermont, New Hampshire, Rhode Island, New York, Massachusetts, Connecticut, Delaware, New Jersey, and of course Washington D.C.

After about 5 years I figure they'll just call France and ask them to invade. Either France or New France will more than likely set a new world record for the fastest surrender in history.

The largest and the one that will survive the longest will be called …. The Consolidated Conservative States of America, TCCSOA. In this new country will be the states of West Virginia, Virginia, Kentucky, Tennessee, North Carolina, South Carolina, Georgia, Florida, Alabama, Mississippi, Louisiana, Texas, Arkansas, Missouri, Oklahoma, Nebraska, Kansas, North Dakota, South Dakota, Montana, Wyoming, Idaho, Alaska, Colorado, New Mexico, Hawaii, Nevada, Utah, and Arizona.

This is the core group who after about 20-25 years will reunite the whole country together again. This group has the resources to feed, and defend their land and people, and the inclination to also do so. After about 3-4 years this country will not have very many problems with illegal immigration. Memphis will be the new capital due to its central location. That and the fact that everyone enjoys going to Graceland for a visit.

We paid a lot of money to get Hawaii to join us, but after a very close vote we decide we wanted to keep a place to park our Navy, and someplace real nice to go on vacation.

We also agreed to keep Nevada in our new country. There was no way we were going to get rid of all of those casinos.

This next country which was named… Rustville United Unionized States of America includes the states of Pennsylvania, Maryland, Indiana, Illinois, Iowa, Ohio, Wisconsin, Michigan, and Minnesota. They will never get their act together, too much in-fighting and after posturing for a few years will end up joining the TCCSOA. But the

TCCSOA only agrees to allow them to join the country if they agree to outlaw all unions.

Now this last group of states which called their country....The New Liberal Left Coast United Acting States.

This country had the states of California, Oregon, and Washington. They wanted Nevada and Utah to join them but they turned them down.

After a few years, they grew tired of California politics, and assassinated their president, some women named Pelosi. Three of the pallbearers turned out to be illegal aliens, 1 of the pallbearers was an out of work actor, and he just kept trying to smile at the cameras, and the other 2 pallbearers were too busy holding hands with each other to do a lot of good.

Someone in the crowd yelled out "Immigration", and they dropped the casket. When the casket hit the ground, it opened up and the body fell out.

Before anyone could do anything about it, the body rolled to the side of the road, and went down in the sewer. Since there were no workers left in the country that could speak English. The body stayed there. As far as anyone knows, to this very day somewhere in San Francisco California, the body of President Pelosi is still in the sewer.

Only a few countries sent people to the funeral services, Cuba, Iran, and North Korea. The Consolidated Conservative States of America, also known as TCCSOA decided to make that day a National Holiday, and President Palin said she was too busy getting ready to go moose hunting to attend the funeral services. They did catch the person who killed her.

He had been released from prison early due to overcrowding, again. He had been in prison 4 times, and had 27 arrests on his record. For killing the President he received a 2 year suspended sentence. But he died a month later, Rosie O'Donnell came to see him in jail and slipped on the floor and landed on him, killing him instantly.

Those conservative states, TCCSOA never once had a problem with people immigrating out of their country, but they still had problems with people wanting to migrate in.


Don't laugh to hard, all of that could come to pass very easily. Think about it, yes some of the states may change but not too many, and the names of the country could change…but not by much.

The only way to stop it from happening will be for the fringe right-wing conservatives to come back from the edge, and get in tune more with the true middle class. Get off of your holier than thou attitude. Quit thinking your opinion is the only one that could possibly be right. Instead of thinking everyone else is stupid and a complete idiot. Perhaps you could look in the mirror a time or two.

If that far right bunch of people would stop spouting off the dribble that they seem to do so often. We would be much better off. I tend to think most times the far right is worse than the far left. And that's a damn shame! What's worse is when the media portrays you that way, and they are so biased in their reporting. They portray the whole Republican Party as such right-wing extremist every time. They know they are doing it, and it feeds right into the Democrats way of doing things.

The way I see this country in its political make up is like this. You have about 15% of the people on the far left-wing.

You'll most likely never change their minds, don't even try it's not going to happen. You have about 15% of the people on the far right-wing. You'll most likely never change their mind, don't even try. These are the groups of people who define their whole parties for the most part. These are also the groups of people in their own parties that are the most dangerous to the rest of their own political parties. Mostly because these are the people the other political parties remember the most and quote the most. It only takes a few stupid comments from a few people for the whole party to look like a bunch of.......extremist, left-wing and right-wing lunatics.

You have about 30% of the people on the middle left and about 30% of the people on the middle right. These are the true middle class of people in this country. These are the ones that work and pay taxes thru the nose, that keep this country going. They are the ones that have no voice in Washington D.C. This group should have the loudest voice there. But they've all-but given up any hope of any real change to our political system. These are the people the government doesn't want to piss off anymore. These are the people who will be voting almost all incumbents out of office in the next 2 elections. (I hope)

The Democrats actually went too far this time, (and for Washington D.C. that's a very hard thing to do) trying to shove health care reform down our throats. With all of the backroom deals, midnight meetings, and of course the cherry on top, a Christmas Eve vote. It was like the Democrats were trying to just get even with Republicans for not passing it when Bill Clinton was in office.

I don't think they even cared what was in the bill. They just wanted to pass a health care reform bill, period. The Cornhusker Shuck, the Louisiana Purchase, call it anything you want to call it, most people I know called it Bullshit.

I'd have to say after losing the Massachusetts Senate seat that was held by Mr. Health Care Reform himself, that a lot of other people decided that they would call it Bullshit too.

That's 90% of the country. The other 10% of the people, the ones who have decided most of the elections for the last 40 or so years. They have no idea how to think for themselves, or can't think for themselves. They simply watch the TV, and internet, and read the newspapers, and they believe whatever is put in front of them. These are the people who are only political when it's popular to be political.

This group of people is more concerned about being popular, and doing what they think is the popular thing to do. This group of people includes the people who complain that certain shows are bad for their children to watch on television. I guess it's just too hard to tell their kids no, you can't watch that show. Of course, don't even think about just changing the channel. I've seen so damn many of these people, when it's not near an election will actually tell people, oh I'm not political, it doesn't matter. But when it gets time to elect someone, they had better belong to their same church, or group of social misfits.

I think if I were the president I would make it mandatory that voters would have to take a competency test before they were allowed to even vote. Wouldn't that be a great thing? If people could not pass a basic test on the issues and on the candidates they could not vote, maybe we could even fine them too. A fine for being stupid, does anyone think that would work? But I guess I'd have to leave that test up to the states. So basically whichever party has the best PR firms or controls the media, wins the elections.

The PR firms/political machines will not be able help either party in the next 2 elections. (But it will not be from a lack of effort)

A lot of incumbents will be surprised in the primary elections this next election, the PR giants will not be able to turn the tide. The Democrats will try to spin it many different ways. But I don't think that many people will buy their trash this time around. Just wait and watch, George Bush and the Republicans will still get blamed for every ailment in this country. PR firms should not be the ones deciding elections in this country. I do not think that was what the founding fathers of this country had in mind.

If all of these countries in the world are so much better than us, why do we always have problems with illegal aliens coming into this country?

You never hear about illegal Americans trying to slip into Mexico for a better life. You never hear about illegal Americans going to Africa for a visit, and are still fighting extradition 4- 5 years later to stay there. I don't recall ever hearing anything about one of George W. Bush's relatives living in this country illegally, and fighting extradition back to Africa. Obama's aunt is still fighting extradition back to Africa 4-5 years after being told NO, and that she needs to go home. Of course it wasn't a big deal before he was elected President.

You never hear about American students going to India to study medicine. I wonder how many American doctors have an office in India? You never hear about American students wanting to go to the Middle East to study engineering. I wonder why? Maybe because most of our buildings are higher than 2 stories, and we have building codes that have to be adhered too. On one of my overseas jobs I was in the U.A.E. There were quite a few engineers there from Egypt. It seemed like almost every time one of them had a problem with someone doing something different than what they had in mind. They had one stock argument for almost every construction related issue. Their argument was, Ahhh, Ahhh, Ahhh, well...... we built the pyramids.

After hearing this a few times, my response back to them was this, well what have you built in the last 4000 years? As an American in the

Middle East, I reserved the right to be rude right back to them. After all we are the terrible American infidels.

I was reading an internet article the other day, and someone placed a quote from Winston Churchill in the comment section. It went something like this. "If you're not a Liberal when your 20 you have no heart, and if you're not a Conservative when your 40 you have no brain." I think it's time we started using our brains more than our hearts.

I have to think in this country that there are a lot more people age 40 and over than there are people aged 18 to 39. Well at least more that vote.

Just because people want to start a grassroots movement doesn't mean they are quacks, or extremist. The way the Democrats and the left-wing media have depicted the Tea- Party people have been absolutely horrendous. I think it is a very symbolic group of people who started that. That's what the founding fathers actually did. That's how this country even came to be. We need a lot more people who will stand up and say, enough is enough. We are to going to take back our government, and our country.

If this ever gets published it should become the Republicans political bible. It could also become a cheat sheet for the Democrats, on how not to lose an election. Both of our idiot political parties should be disbanded and outlawed. Why don't we just call them by their real names anyway? Instead of Democrat and Republican, let's just call them what they are the Liberals and the Conservatives. And hell that's not even real accurate. Maybe the most accurate party names should be the Liars and Crooks Party and the Holier than Thou and Liars Party.

The Liberal politicians just lie and twist facts around till they get something they like.

They don't seem to care about facts, or historical conclusions, or even history. The only time anything from past history gets brought into a conversation, is when they try to blame the Republicans for something else.

I don't really think the Speaker of the House needs her own airplane, especially a jumbo jet to fly her and her staff back and forth between California and Washington D.C. You want to talk about eliminating some waste? Another thing, how in the hell did she ever become The Speaker of the House? If I were running things, that voting process would have been shown on C-Span for the whole country to see.

The so called Conservative politicians are not a lot better. It's hard to convince people you're a Conservative when you live in multi-million dollar mansions, and you need to go to Hawaii for a political conference. Washington D.C. is a long long way from Maui. Also you need to get out of big businesses pocket. That's not where you'll find conservative ideas or people.

Americans don't care if someone gets rich, hell that's the American Dream. Where you lose the real people, the real Conservatives, are the multi-million dollar bonuses that people in the big corporations get for losing billions of dollars. They lost the money because they got greedy.

Big daddy government is also not allowed to bail out losers, any of them, ever, period! That's the free market system.

If they were too big to fail, then Washington politicians let that happen too. They've been breaking up monopolies for years, oil companies, the phone company, even Microsoft. I along with a lot of other people do not believe any company is too big to fail. The only thing that should be too big to fail is the United States of America. But Washington D.C. decides it is better for our country to have a massive debt, than to let companies that were stupid go out of business.

Hell, why not just bail out every homeowner who is behind in their house payment? Why not bail out everyone who is behind in their car payment? Why not bail out everybody who is behind on their credit cards? Why, because it's not the American way.

There are a few other reasons that our government would never do something like that. First no matter which party was in power the other party would never allow it to happen because the party in power that did it would have a real landslide in the next election. Another reason would be that the politicians would not be able to get any kickbacks this way.

You see you politicians have screwed the American people for so long, even if you didn't get kickbacks from the banks, automakers/ unions, and Wall Street we will always believe you did. The reasons that the politicians used in giving all of those banks, automakers/ unions, and Wall Street those bailouts are the exact same reason they use to not give real Americans the very same thing.

Let me try and explain my thoughts on this subject. The reasons the politicians gave more than a Trillion dollars of our money to help shore up all of those businesses was that the economy needed help. We were told if these businesses failed then our whole economy/country could collapse.

We bailed out a lot of businesses. What about the companies that did not get bailed out? What incentive did they or do they have to keep doing business? They've seen our government bail out their competitors when they ran their companies into the ground. I think every company in America that did not receive any bailout money should sue the federal government. I think they could win too. What makes one company better than the next one? But that is why we could never just pay off peoples mortgages that were/are behind on their payments.

If we paid off just the people who were behind on their payments, what incentive is it for the rest of us who are not behind in our payments to keep making our payments? If the government is going to pay off everyone's mortgage, why not pay off everyone's credit card too? If they're going to pay off everyone's mortgage and credit cards, why not pay off everyone's vehicles also?

I would like to see our government waste another couple of hundred million dollars to do a study. Just to see if they would have spent more money or less money on bailing out every Americans mortgage, credit card bills, and vehicle payoffs.

Or bailing out Wall Street, automakers/unions, and the banks?

I can guaranty you one thing, if they had bailed out the American people, there would have been a lot more jobs created and a lot more happy people. Everybody would still be buying things, because they all would still have jobs and money.

Am I wrong, or do the bailouts and all of that stuff kind of sound a lot like trickledown economics? You remember that term from Ronald Reagan, a dead Republican President, who the Democrats still fear. Now a Democrat Party President is emulating a Republican President.

Does anyone still remember how the Democrats bashed and made fun of that trickledown economy at the time? It took awhile for it to work, but it did work. It only took Bill Clinton about 6 years to ruin it. Some people think the very first day a new President steps into the White House everything that happens, and is good is that Presidents doing. They also think everything that happens and is bad, is the last Presidents fault.

I keep hearing how Bill Clinton was the last American President to have a balanced budget. That is just so such bullshit.

It took Reagan and Bush, 12 years to clean up Jimmy Carter's crappy economy, and pitiful foreign policy failures and to get America back on track on the world stage and to get the American economy going again. It only took 5 ½ to 6 years for the Democrats to bring it all back down again. Clinton's last 2 years or so, the economy was heading straight into the toilet. Entitlement programs for the inter-city poor and for the minorities, and raising taxes for the working class of this nation, I think have been proven to be, not the way to go. The Democrats, I think would cease to exist if they had to be in power for longer than 8-12 years in a row.

I think there a few striking similarities between Clinton and Obama. The most glaring is the fact I do not think anyone really thought that they would win their first presidential elections when they first started to run for President. I think they both were being prepped for name recognition on the national stage, and they both just caught on fire at the right time and won, despite themselves.

With Bill Clinton, it was simple, Ross Perot handed it to him in a gift wrapped election. Perot was never going to get any of the Democrats votes. He simple took votes away from Bush.

With Obama, it was a little more complicated, but not much. Hillary Clinton, simple forgot she needed to run an election. Who could possibly run against her on the Democrats side? I personally think there was a deal cut with her and the Democratic Party. If she stayed with Bill and didn't divorce him, they would support her Senate run and then a run at the White House. Her primaries were supposed to be just about bashing Bush and the Republicans.

She was 1/2 way thru the primaries before she even knew there was someone else running on the Democratic ticket. Everyone else was supposed to implode before she reached Super Tuesday. She thought she had the black vote in the bag.

Then she realized that there was a black guy running, who wasn't Jesse Jackson. By then it was already too late to do anything about it. He had already woken up the black people to vote in mass. Coupled with the fact, a lot of people hated anyone named Clinton. With groups like Acorn getting every inter-city black and minority to register to vote, and I believe more than a few times getting them to register more than once.

As a Republican voter in that election, it was almost comical watching her flounder around. She didn't know what to do. She couldn't utter a word about him being unqualified to be president, because she wasn't qualified.

She couldn't make any kind of comments about his race. That's because her base of voters were the same as his, the black people. The Democratic Party wasn't going to allow any kind of fighting within their own party this time around. Because they knew they had a chance to ride a big wave of success in both houses of congress as well as the Whitehouse.

When she did finally wake up and realized it was most likely to late to do anything about it, she had to hedge her bet and try to weasel her way in somehow. After McCain picked Sarah Palin as a running mate, and Obama starting losing some ground in the polls, Hillary grabbed her last straw.

She decided she would endorse Obama in exchange for a nice Cabinet post. The Democrats could not pass up a chance to see their 2 big dogs strolling hand in hand across that stage.

Obama couldn't offer her the Vice Presidents spot. Because I believe he just didn't want her and Bill anywhere near the White House again, and looking over his shoulder. I'm not real sure he even trusted her. The rumor mill has it, that the Clintons could make people disappear that tended to disagree with them and for people who knew things about them. But that's just something I read on the internet.

With George W. Bush leaving office with the economy heading south, and an overseas war that was and is still not going anywhere. Disgruntled people wanted to believe Obama and his lies about hope and change. Some people actually believe what they see and hear on TV and read on the internet. I believe what most people were saying to the Democrats was this, OK we'll listen to you and give you a chance. But you had better be telling the truth. Most of the white people I know would have no problem voting for a black person. We don't really care what color they are, but we do think they should qualified for the job.

My biggest problem with Obama when he was running for President was the fact he never said anything. He just kept saying how bad the Republicans were doing it. Anyone with even half a brain should know that you can't promise and deliver everything to everyone. To me the election was simply about affirmative action. The liberals finally had a chance to make up for white people in this country owning slaves 200 years ago. I don't think anyone, regardless of their skin color are entitled to anything, much less the presidency. The media refused for the most part, to say anything critical of him for fear of someone using the race card.

The media should have made such a stink about Obama's preacher that he would not have been able to run for dog catcher, even in Chicago. Obama going to that church for 20 years or so with that preacher should have been no different than if people found out that McCain was going to Klu Klux Klan meetings for 20 years. They could find paper on George Bush from 40 years ago, but they can't find this guys passport, or birth certificate, or even his collage transcripts? This is a person who is running for President of the United States, not a city council job in Jerkwater USA.

George Bush was fair game for anything. Hell, McCain was not even in the race till he picked Sarah Palin as a running mate, and he did that just to try and get the women's vote since the Democrats picked Obama over Hillary.

I have never seen an election where one person was running against another person who was not even seeking the job. The election was Obama against Bush, and Bush couldn't even run for another term. I also believe McCain sought to distance himself from Bush.... well he did. One was a 2 term President. The other is a Senator from Arizona who could not win a national election, and helped his political party lose both houses of Congress.

A lot of people will and have been faced with losing their homes recently. A lot of those people should have never been in the home they were in. I place blame for the shady home loan debacle squarely on the Democrats shoulders. Bill Clinton is the one to blame for most of them. He's the one who had made the Freddie Mack's and the Fannie Mae's loosen up their purse strings on home buying requirements for low income earners and for minorities.

This is typical of the Democrats trying to act like they were helping minorities become home owners.

The problem that was created was the fact that the home that they should have been able to purchase was not located where they wanted it to be, or was not the homes that they wanted.

If a married couple with 2 kids wanted to buy a house, fine. He makes 40,000 a year, she makes 25,000 a year. They have 2 cars 1 is paid off, the other has a monthly note, say 300 a month. They have a couple of credit cards, say another 300 a month bill. By the time you figure all of the other monthly bills, light bill, water, cable, cell phones, insurance, life and car, food, cloths, rent, and all the dozens of other things we all have to pay for. Now you get to add in house insurance and taxes also.

Their credit score is not too bad, but not great either. They should have been looking at homes in the 30,000 to 50,000 dollar range. But they got hooked up with some special financing terms, and now all of a sudden they're being told, we can put you in this real nice 225,000 dollar house. They never even dreamed they could ever afford a house like that.

Great schools in the area, low crime area, good area of town, nice parks nearby. They were right. If something sounds too good to be true, it usually is. Maybe they didn't read the fine print or maybe they were told to adjust their incomes upwardly, and then they could qualify for their new home.

It doesn't matter they should have never been in that house. Then it all starts to come undone, they ran up their credit cards buying new furniture and for a few new thing to go in that house. The wife wants to trade in that old car. The kids are getting bigger they'll need more room soon, so now they have a nice SUV, and another car note.

About 6 months later she gets laid off from work, it's happening all over the place. Well the next thing you know they're getting further and further behind on their bills. They've already borrowed money from every place and everybody they can borrow from. The phone calls from bill collectors are coming more often now. So now they've been in their new house for about 2 years. There is no way in hell they can make the house payments now. They've already had the SUV repossessed.

They get the notice from the finance company that they have started foreclosure proceedings on the house.

The Democrats use them as an example of the people who need help keeping their homes. They are blaming the Republicans and pointing out the fat-cat bankers who have gotten bail outs and are still receiving multi-million dollar bonuses. Neither of which have anything to do with them making their house payment.

The Republicans use them as an example of how the Democrats loosening up regulations put people like this in a house that they should have never been in the first place.

Well I've got news for both parties, you're both right and you're both wrong. Congress does this a lot; I wonder sometimes if it is not planned that way too? On this issue I do have to lean toward the Republicans being more right than wrong. Just being a minority, is not reason enough to be put in a home that they cannot afford. Owning one's own home should still be a huge part of the American dream.

Sometimes neither the lender nor the buyer does anything wrong or even underhanded.

I knew a couple that had been married for around 25 years. They decide that they needed to get divorced. The reasons do not matter, but they got divorced. When they purchased the home, together they made around 150,000-160,000 dollars a year, and had almost perfect credit. He made about 60,000 she made about 100,000. They had 2 children in collage, and 2 still at home.

During this economic recession her work hours were cut down somewhat. So instead of her making 100,000 dollars a year, she now only makes around 80,000 dollars a year. Yes still a very nice living, but not near what "they" were making when they bought the house.

Not many people can survive a 50% cut in income when they have a 2000 dollar a month house payment. And of course a few months into the divorce her car blows an engine, so now she even has a car note, something she hasn't had in awhile.

One of her kids has to quit collage. She can't even find a job that pays enough to go to college on. The other one was in his last year, which ended up taking 2 years because he had to get another job to pay for school. With the real estate market going down the tubes, she lost all of the equity in the house that had built up the last 15 years. She treaded water for awhile before finally just giving the house up.

But she was foreclosed on just the same as the minority couple was. She even got hurt by Bill Clinton and the Democrats helping the minorities getting into their house. By them getting foreclosed on in so many places, that was the key to the real estate market going in the tank. Had that not been happening in many places all over the country. The woman who lost her home would have been able to sell her home, and take the equity that had built up in the house and buy another less expensive home. That would have in turn helped keep the economy flowing and helped keep people employed.

That's why the government needs to stay out of the bail-out business.

If they had let those big companies fail, other more efficient companies would have taken their places. That's what needs to happen to the car companies also. I do not want a stake in Government Motors.

Politicians should have to account for every single dollar that they make while they are in an elected position in this country. Also for 10 years after they leave office. They should have to divest all of their stocks and bonds before being sworn in. It would need to be put in a (real) blind trust. Even better yet, all Democrats would have to take all of their money, stocks, and bonds, and invest it in just regular stock at GM.

All Republicans would have to invest all of theirs in common stock with AIG. I wonder how that would go over in both houses of Congress?

I would put a cap on how much all political races could have spent on them. I would cap how many commercials each candidate could run on TV, internet, and on the radio. I would make it mandatory that in any political race the candidates would have to meet for a debate, and in the area that they were running in, and each person would each get half of the tickets to the event.

It is completely stupid to spend 10 million dollars for a job that last for 2 years, and pays 200,000 a year.

And people wonder why we have a 14 trillion dollar deficit. I would put a limit of 1/10th of their annual salary in the job that they are running for.

There are 4 mainstream broadcast channels for the most part, NBC, CBS, ABC, and FOX. Each candidate gets to run 1 commercial a week on each channel. You can only start running them 30 days before the election date. The networks would have to run them for free. All of them would have to be run at the same time and on the same days. In other words the Democrats don't get theirs on the air at 7:00 pm on Tuesday night on CBS, and the Republicans at 3:00 am.

We could make every other Monday night and every other Thursday night, political candidate commercial night at 8pm during the election cycles.

For those of you who say the networks will never do it, wrong again. If they ever want to cover anything at the White House again they will.

If they want to renew their FCC license they will. If they want their satellites to keep working or even get them into space they will.

Donations to political candidates would be controlled more carefully. I think a donation cap of 5000 dollars should be plenty. Donations could be accepted from individuals only, and they could only come from within the same state as the person running.

Then only with proper documentation, like prove of citizenship. If rich individuals wanted to be more involved in the election process, that's fine, to a certain extent. If someone like Bill Gates wants to provide a jet plane to a Senate candidate who he likes, that's fine. But he would have to also provide the same plane for the same amount of time to the other candidate, at no cost or the same cost.

It's time to take special interest out of politics. Candidates need to run on their own merits, not what they can do for a few privileged people. Senators and member of the House of Representatives should be held accountable to people in their own state, not to a particular political party. The president needs to be held accountable to the American people and to America not to any political party.

We as Americans have allowed this to happen. It took many many years for it to happen. That's why most people never saw it happen. I'm not even sure when it started. I don't know that anyone does. Some say it started with FDR, some say it was Lincoln, some say Nixon. But one thing I do know, it's time to stop it. Sometimes things are just too broke to fix, and I think our Congress is to broke to fix right now. It's time to throw it out and start over.

I think it could be done without disrupting our country too badly.

After all, other than their own families I don't think anyone really likes any of them. The stock market might jump around a little bit, and some other countries might jump up and down a little bit, but I don't think anything to bad.

Most of the other countries that would be doing the most jumping would be the ones that were going to be losing out from the new United States of America. I think we would be seeing a lot traveling from a lot of people heading south thru Texas and California. The stock market would calm down after a few weeks, then most likely start going up.

Everything would not be perfect overnight. It would take awhile for all of the changes to happen and happen correctly. But after getting the right people in the right jobs, which is very important by the way. Things would start to happen. The key to being a good manager is to get the right people in the right jobs, then have enough sense to let them do their jobs. Not everyone is cut out to be a manager. I would trim so much government waste it would be pitiful. People would look back and say, "Damn" …..why did that take so long to happen?

I would make every member of both houses of Congress put all of their money that they have made since they've been elected into a special fund. (outside of their salary)That fund would then be given to the state that elected them. I would like to make them all retire at the age of 65 and live off of social security. I would also like to make it mandatory that no one could serve in any of the 3 branches of government unless they had served in some branch of the military. I would make an exemption for certain types of handicaps. Physical ones, not mental ones, we have far too many mental cases in Washington D.C. now.

Has anyone else noticed that the President has never stopped campaigning? Most people who win an election to a four year job would not feel a need to campaign for the entire four years. At some point you would think he would try and do his job. By the way, getting other Democrats elected in November is not his job. The President of the United States should be able to be above politics. It seems the only way this one can get his poll numbers to go in an upwardly direction is for him to get out of the White House. I don't even think the people that voted for him, planned for him to still be on the campaign trail.

I can see him sticking his nose into the special Massachusetts Senate race for a few days, maybe a speech or two, but not a lot more than that.

Contrary to the Democratic believe, the name Obama does not carry the weight of an automatic victory. Sometimes in life, sort of like a real job, you actually have to do something, or get something done. Standing around and reading from a teleprompter what your liberal lap-dogs have told you what to say is not a skill that is very much in need of.

Please give me a break on the so called town hall meetings. The Democrat's idea of a town hall meeting for their leader is to pack a small building in a small town and only let in people they choose. Of course they pick a city mostly with either a very heavy Democratic base and or an urban area. (same thing) This way they can pick which questions from which people he will get to answer.

If the damn Republicans and the news media would stop playing with this guy and quit being afraid of offending a black person, then maybe someone would actually ask some serious questions of him.

The Republicans should not be so enamored with their recent success in elections either. They are setting themselves up for a huge letdown come election time. The biggest reason that the Republicans won a few Governor jobs and the one Senate seat is twofold. First there was not a black person running, therefore the large black voter turnout was not there. It will be back when Obama runs again in 2012. The second reason is the fact that the Democrats are completely ineffective as national leaders. They do not know or care enough to govern for the entire country. All they have cared about so far is getting back at the Republicans and George Bush.

I have a news flash for you idiot Democrats; George W. Bush is no longer the president. Also he cannot run again, get over him. Quit sticking pins in your George W. Bush doll. The Democrat's other wants and needs have nothing to do with a national policy. Their wants and needs have to do with Democrats.

The Democratic Party is as diverse as the Republican Party is, if not even more so. The Democrats had the perfect storm as far as the Republicans were concerned. They had the White House, they had the Senate, and they had the House of Representatives all at the same time. They even had a super majority in the Senate, a filibuster prove majority.

With all of that at their finger tips, they could not agree on their signature piece of legislation.

Only after they lost their super majority in the Senate did the Democrats even try to blame the Republicans for not helping them with the legislation. The Republicans who had been totally shutout of the backroom deals and midnight meetings were now at fault for not playing bipartisan politics. The Republicans were told by Obama shortly after the election, so I heard, and I believe, "that there are consequences to every election, and you lost and we won this one, so get used to it".

Every time the Democrats get on TV, they only want to talk about the lack of bipartisan politics on the Republicans part. I have to wonder if anyone really believes this dribble? They control the White House and both houses of Congress. Does anyone really think that the Democrats have even tried to get the Republicans to do anything other than to swallow what they tell them that they are going to pass? I always thought a compromise involved two sides giving a little. Maybe we should call the U.N. and request a group of foreign peace keepers to come to Washington D.C. and restore order?

Something or somebody has to change the way it is now.

If the Democrats say its nighttime outside, the Republicans will say ....no it's not, it's evening or just late in the day. If the Republicans say its daytime the Democrats will say.....no its not, and the sun is out because of Republican backed global warming, and George W. Bush is behind it all. And Dick Chaney is trying to cover it up.

Since a certain President was able to get away with lying while being under oath, and making people define the word sex, Washington D.C. has been able to get away with anything they want to.

I defy any open minded person to refute anything I've stated in here!

I defy any open minded person to tell me one thing in here that I've stated that cannot happen! Out of all of the things in here, I think the hardest thing to get accomplished would be getting every member of Congress arrested after the military coup. I have to wonder how many of the liberal left-wingers would seek political asylum in Cuba or North Korea? Couldn't you just see Nancy Pelosi asking for asylum from Castro?

Now I know that most, if not all that I have written about will never take place. Most if not all that I have written about should happen in this country. If it were to happen, then this country would truly be the land of the free and the home of the brave.

The word manifesto has become synonymous with radicals and extremist. What with people flying planes into buildings and going on killing sprees. That's not what this book is all about. This book is about changes that need to happen in this country for this country to survive.

# THE END.......?